HEROES
◆F THE
FAITH

LOGAN AMES

WORLDVIEW WARRIORS
PUBLISHING

Formatted and edited by Katie Erickson
Cover and interior artwork by Scott Harshbarger

ISBN: 9781792744488

DEDICATION

To my Lord and Savior, Jesus Christ, who loved me and pursued me when I didn't even care, and who continues to sanctify me by his unlimited power and grace.

To my amazing wife, Clara. You encourage me to follow God's call, love me unconditionally, and hold me accountable with truth and grace. And to our precious daughter, Evangeline. You make me want to be a better man and I can't wait to watch you grow into the woman you were created to be.

To my loving parents, Sheldon and Debbie, and all who helped to raise me and teach me to trust and honor God in all circumstances. I am forever grateful that God gave me each of you. I know how truly blessed I am!

PUBLISHER'S NOTE

In the decision making process of this book, early on we knew we wanted our friend and artist, Scott Harshbarger of The Art of Harsh, to not only do the interior illustrations of this book but the cover art as well. We think he has hit a home run with all of these illustrations but specifically with the cover. We here at Worldview Warriors are truly all in awe. We gave him the idea of what we wanted, but he took it so much farther than we even imagined.

As you can see, it is Moses and the Israelites crossing the Red Sea. In this image, they have already crossed the Red Sea and God is continuing to fight for them in the pillar of the cloud against the Egyptian army, even into the Red Sea itself. Go read the passage this image is based on to help you to visualize these events even more in Exodus 14. In verse 27, you can see that the Lord is fighting for the Israelites even into the sea. Personally, I still get chills when I see this image.

We hope this book helps you to see who the real hero is in this creation. It's Almighty God, Creator of heaven and earth. He works in and through those who are willing to hear His voice and obey. Thanks for reading this resource, and we hope it encourages and equips you to serve God in all that you do.

–Jason DeZurik
Worldview Warriors President

TABLE OF CONTENTS

Introduction
Remember the Heroes

We all have heroes. The word gets used too often to describe celebrities, star athletes, and politicians who are concerned with power and money over using their platform to help and inspire others. Heroism generally has less to do with fame and more to do with extraordinary moments or events. For the generation before me, it may have been Billy Graham, Martin Luther King, Jr., or Neil Armstrong. While their names have become known, their common goal was not fame but to do something extraordinary with the opportunities presented to them. In my lifetime, heroes have been ordinary, everyday human beings who were put in unbelievable situations and overcame evil and fear to do the work of the Lord, including the saving of lives.

Many of the heroes that come to my mind showed their resilience and courage on September 11, 2001. Thousands were murdered at the hands of terrorists who hijacked airplanes and flew them into the World Trade Center buildings, the Pentagon, and a rural field in Pennsylvania no more than 50 miles from where I was living and going to college at the time. In some ways, it feels like it was just yesterday. In other ways, it feels like a lifetime ago.

While many people recognize the heroism we all witnessed that day and in the months that followed in efforts to save lives or rescue those trapped, we are certainly apt to forget about it. With each passing year, it feels like more and more of a distant or fading memory. We love to declare the catch phrase, "Never forget." Yet, that's exactly what has happened as we've gotten further away from that day. Other than the locations where the planes went down (and even in those places, it's only once a year), there is very little intentional remembrance regarding the heroism of that day.

For many, the reason we remember events like 9/11 is because they remind us of the presence of evil in our world, our own mortality, and our need for better vetting of potential terrorists. However, I feel we are missing the big picture if those are the only things we choose to remember about that day. In the Old Testament, God frequently told the Israelites to DO things to make sure they remember his goodness and faithfulness toward them. These included observing very specific instructions regarding Passover as a "lasting ordinance" (**Exodus 12:24-28**), remembering the Sabbath as a day to rest, stop, and think about all that God has given them (**Exodus 20:8-11**), and taking twelve stones from the middle of the Jordan River after God stopped it from flowing temporarily so they could cross into the Promised Land (**Joshua 4:1-7**). Each of these things required the Israelites to be intentional. If they relied on randomly celebrating or commemorating God's faithfulness, they'd eventually lose sight of it.

When I think back to the events surrounding that fateful day of September 11, 2001, which is one of the most memorable dates in this country's history, I believe it's absolutely critical for us to remember not only that we are mere mortals who rely on God's grace and protection every moment of every day, but also the positive things that took place in the midst of tragedy. Our nation was very divided politically back then, but suddenly the pain brought us all back to reality and gave us a greater purpose than arguing. We were reminded to band together, to seek unity, and to love unconditionally. As our nation has witnessed the devastation of more terrorist attacks and natural disasters since that day, we have continued to be reminded of these things in the midst of our dysfunction and political arguing. We have also seen ordinary people risking their lives to save others in every one of these incidents just as they did on September 11, 2001, and I believe we should intentionally reflect on the sacrifices and bravery of so many first responders who rushed into the falling towers on September 11 and the flooding waters during storms to save people they didn't even know.

Think about the men and women on board Flight 93 that went down in Shanksville, PA. Think about the first responders who ran toward danger on September 11. Think about those who swam or waded in rushing waters to save people during the hurricanes and floods. Think about the former Navy SEAL from Thailand who gave his life and many from our nation who gave their time trying to save a youth soccer team trapped in a flooded cave in 2018. I believe we should be intentional about remembering all of these heroes because God worked through all of them, ordinary people who, when called upon, did extraordinary things. We must remember them as examples for us, so that when we are called upon to do the extraordinary, we might trust God and be His vessels as they were.

While I've written about reflecting on the heroism shown during these trying times in our history, remembering heroes is just as important in the Bible. This book is filled with heroes we find in **Hebrews 11**. Why was it important for the writer of Hebrews to specifically talk about all of those people and what they were able to accomplish by faith? I believe it's for the same reason that God emphasized remembering in the Old Testament. The word "remember" has roots that mean "to recall to mind." For the Hebrew believers, many of them were familiar with the stories that we find in **Hebrews 11**. But maybe they struggled to find hope and faith for themselves. Maybe as they faced difficult circumstances, they were unable to recall to mind how God had so mightily moved in the lives of others. They needed the reminder and the encouragement to stand strong in their faith no matter how dark or tragic things may appear.

I believe the same is true for you and me. We need to think about and remember the heroes of our faith just as we remember the contemporary heroes during our lifetime. The heroes of our faith, referred to as "witnesses" in **Hebrews 12:1**, were ordinary men and women. They did not have some super faith. They had average faith in a super God. Jesus Christ is the ultimate hero of our Christian faith, but when ordinary men and women trusted in Him even when the odds said they would likely be destroyed by their circumstances, they prevailed in extraordinary ways. Through their faith, God gave them confidence and assurance of things that they couldn't envision, and the Word tells us they were "commended" for that faith (**Hebrews 11:1-2**).

As we go through their stories, you're going to want to grab a Bible and follow along. Take some time to read over their original stories as we prepare to dig into them one-by-one. Be intentional about picking out specific stories or details that most apply to whatever you're currently going through. As we intentionally recall to mind how they prevailed in the faith, we can also find confidence and assurance of God's victory in our times of need.

CHAPTER 1
UNDERSTANDING BY FAITH

When you're afraid of something in life, how do you overcome it? Do you essentially just close your eyes and wait for the circumstances to pass you by, hoping that you won't get harmed? Do you "man up" or "woman up" and face them head on?

Personally, I rarely take either of those two approaches. God has given me a very analytical mind, so it causes me to approach my fears differently than many people. While others might take the "try not to think about it" path, I gave up on that idea a long time ago. I must find a way to reason in my own head that I'll be okay.

When I was afraid of roller coasters as a child, I watched happy and healthy people with all of their limbs intact walking off *The Sidewinder* at Hersheypark in Hershey, Pennsylvania, and I reasoned that I would not be injured or killed because they were not. Even when I went skydiving as an adult in 2005, I was terrified, yet I reasoned that the odds for survival were in my favor based on seeing other people successfully complete their jumps and knowing that a very large majority of people who do it survive and love it!

In the church, so often we respond to legitimate questions or fears that people have with some form of, "That's why they call it faith." Sometimes, that might be an appropriate response. Other times, it's an incredibly lazy one. How can followers of Christ expect to develop other potential believers by pretending as if the entire foundation of our belief system is blind faith? If we look at Scripture, there are few circumstances where God requires us to trust Him with no basis or foundation whatsoever.

As I mentioned before, God routinely commanded His people in the Bible to intentionally remember what He had done for them in the past. This wasn't because God needed some kind of pat on the back; God doesn't need our approval, our thanks, or our encouragement. The purpose for God telling them to be intentional about remembering what He did for them and how He showed up for them over and over again when they would have otherwise been destroyed was to show them they had REASON to keep trusting Him.

Faith is not the opposite of reason. Some people say that faith in an unseen God defies logic, but I guess that all depends on what your standard of reason is. As we embark on a journey that will cause us to look at each and every one of the heroes of our faith mentioned in **Hebrews 11**, including some who are not mentioned by name, we must understand that they trusted God because their standard of reason had been altered.

Before addressing any of the specific individuals, the writer of the chapter gives us what I believe is the foundational verse for the whole thing: "By faith we understand that the universe was formed at God's command, so that what is seen was not made out of what was visible" (**Hebrews 11:3**). This is a verse you will see quite a bit throughout this book. The men and women of this chapter who put their lives in the hands of their Creator did so with more than a blind and unreasonable belief that He was worthy of their confidence. It was an established truth that they UNDERSTOOD.

We, too, can have that understanding by faith when we face impossible and trying circumstances. Let's follow the same logic the writer and most likely the heroes in Hebrews 11 did. If you walk outside right now and look up at the stars, down at the flowers, around at the mountains, or out toward the beaches and oceans, you basically have two choices in deciding how you believe it all came to be as it is. You either believe that someone designed it that way, or you believe that it happened by some stroke of luck or chance. Maybe you believe that chance has been accurately described by scientific research, but if so, there is still uncertainty involved because you'd have to decide where the very first form of matter originated.

Do you realize that either of the two options I described above requires faith? Since we can't be 100% sure either way, it's a matter of faith. If you believe that someone designed what we see outside, then you must decide if it's the God of the Bible or someone else.

This is where faith and understanding go hand in hand. The beginning of the Bible in Genesis tells us all about what God created. Then we go outside and can physically see with our very eyes that it's designed just as the Word says it is. Even later in **Genesis 9**, we see that God created the rainbow for a purpose. Today, we can still walk outside and occasionally see the rainbow as God created it.

God's not asking you to trust Him just because He says so. He's saying, "Look around and understand that you can trust me." Continuing with the logic of the writer of Hebrews, if God could make everything that we see out of what was not visible, is there anything He can't handle? We must understand how small our view of God is and how limited our view of his involvement in our circumstances can be at times.

If our standard of reasoning through our difficult circumstances is only extended as far as we can have control over them, then we won't be able to trust God for anything. If our best doctors in the world say there is nothing they can do for a patient with a terminal illness, then we have no reason to have hope. On the flip side, if our standard of reasoning BEGINS with the understanding that God absolutely created everything that we see out of what was not visible, then the things for which we need His intervention seem like small potatoes in comparison. That terminal illness for which there is no cure could easily be healed by God. That drug addiction which has a grip on you or your loved one is nothing compared to God's love and strength. Those attacks by your enemies don't stand a chance against God's power.

In a world with increasing uncertainty, we must stand on the only thing we know IS certain: hope and trust in God. We've had major hurricanes, continued terror attacks all over the world, political unrest, and threats of nuclear war. These seem like overwhelming and troubling circumstances to face, and they don't even include whatever you are facing in your personal life. Left to our own reasoning, fear will overtake us. But when we think about what we know God has already created and accomplished, we are able to reason that He can do what we need and much more.

I encourage you to compare the miracles you need from Him to creating the world out of what we can't see, and let your understanding by faith be your guide to get through whatever it is. Do that today, and let's begin together to look at other men and women just like us who had to go through the same reasoning process.

CHAPTER 2
THE FAITH OF ABEL

If you have a sibling with whom you are very close, chances are that you've had moments in your life when you felt like you were doing everything right and still got the shaft. You probably felt that your parents favored your brother or sister and that just really irked you. I remember when I turned 16 years old and was eager to get my driver's license. However, I already had my own car and it had a manual transmission. Because of this, my parents made me learn how to drive stick shift before I was allowed to get my license. Two years later, my younger brother turned 16 and was allowed to get his license right away even though he had no vehicle and had to share my mom's car. This annoyed me and seemed unfair! Eventually, I got over it because ultimately, it could only affect me if I let it. Plus, there's always the fact that it was a completely immature view of things. My parents had good reasons for their decisions.

Most of us grow out of these feelings, yet there are some who allow them to grow into a bitter root that ultimately consumes them. That's been going on for almost as long as human beings have been around on this planet. In this chapter, we'll learn about someone who allowed his jealousy and selfish feelings to overpower him, as well as someone who didn't focus on such petty things because his focus and faith were in the Lord.

Our foundational verse for this book about our faithful heroes is **Hebrews 11:3**, which says, "By faith, we understand that the universe was formed at God's command, so that what is seen was not made out of what was visible." With this understanding of what God was able to accomplish as our foundation, the miracles we need seem entirely possible and our complaints seem all the more pointless.

We see in the next verse that the first person mentioned by the writer of Hebrews as one who was faithful is Abel. You can read

Genesis 4 on your own and see that Abel is the younger brother of Cain, and they were the first two sons of Adam and Eve.

In **Hebrews 11:4**, we're told that Abel's faith caused him to bring a "better offering" to God than Cain did. Right off the bat, that makes us a little uncomfortable because we are comparing something that seems like it shouldn't be compared. I mean, none of us would approve of someone sitting and judging one person's offering at church as "better" than someone else's. But the NIV translation of the Bible doesn't give us anything else to go with. Take a look at the same verse in The Message: "By an act of faith, Abel brought a better sacrifice to God than Cain. It was what he *believed*, not what he *brought*, that made the difference. That's what God noticed and approved as righteous. After all these centuries, that belief continues to catch our notice." It wasn't just about what they brought to the Lord, because the Lord also knew their hearts, and Abel's offering was based on faith. If we go back to Genesis 4, we see that Abel and Cain had separate jobs that they did, they each brought offerings to the Lord, and the Lord favored Abel's offering but not Cain's (**vv. 3-5**). The question is, why?

Let me go ahead and put the disclaimer out there that anytime we are trying to dig into the mind of God, we should tread carefully, especially if the answer is not crystal clear in Scripture. In this case, however, we can gain an understanding with a little deeper look into **Genesis 4:3-5**. These verses tell us that Cain brought SOME of the fruits of his soil, while Abel brought fat portions from the firstborn of his flock. This may seem insignificant, but their actions reveal a little bit about their hearts. Cain's offering appears to have been a little more reluctant than Abel's. We don't know that for certain, but we do know that he brought "some" of what the Lord provided for him. In other words, he gave God his leftovers. Abel, however, gave the fat portions (considered to be the most luxurious part of the meat) of the firstborn of his flock. This means that before he took anything for himself, he gave the very best that he had to the Lord.

As I said earlier, the Lord knew each man's heart. So, we can't say for sure that his favor was based only on the nature of the offering. But this does teach us something about our own attitudes toward our giving. Do we recognize that God has given us literally everything we have? Does that even matter to us? When we decide to give back to him through the local church or in other ways, is it something that we do out of religious necessity only after we have taken care of everything we want first? Or do we offer to God the very best of what we've been given because, by faith, we trust Him to meet all of our other needs? These are the questions we must answer individually, and how we answer them says a lot about our faith.

You can read the rest of the story in Genesis 4 to see what transpired. In short, Cain is angry and sad about God not accepting his offering. He is given the chance by God to master his own emotions, repent, and choose to do what is right. He doesn't, so his emotions lead him to a fit of jealousy and rage in which he kills his own brother. The Lord confronts him and he lies, even mocking God in the process. Then he gets a persecution complex and believes that everyone will be out to get him for the rest of his life. We never see any sign that Cain repents in any way.

Cain's sinful choices began with emotions, which by themselves are not necessarily considered "sin." God spoke to him at a critical moment when the temptation to act out of his sin was strong and urged him to master that temptation. But Cain gave into it and became a murderer, only one generation after sin entered the world. While Abel is our faith hero for the week, we read very little about him. Why is that?

Friends, doing the right thing in God's eyes won't get you much fame or attention. But when your actions are lined up against the actions of those who do not follow Him or live by faith, you'll be an example to others. Depending on the situation God puts you in, you might even get the chance to be a witness to the whole world. Abel was a human being. I'm sure he was tempted to sin just as Cain was. But his proper perspective on who God is caused him to make his faith his first priority. It wasn't just about what Abel believed intellectually, but more so about how his beliefs translated to action.

What is God asking you to do by faith? What sins are in your life that you recognize desperately want to have power over you? If you believe that God created the entire universe out of nothing as the Word says He did, then let that faith influence how you approach every area of your life, including giving, resisting sin, and letting God be your defender when someone is jealous or bitter toward you. Let's learn from Abel's example and apply it to our own lives.

Chapter 3
The Faith of Enoch

If you grew up in the church or knew someone who did, you have likely heard a pastor or someone reference a poem called "Footprints in the Sand." It's popular on social media as well. The poem is written from the standpoint of someone who is dreaming they are walking along the beach with the Lord. In Christianity, the phrase "walk with God" is something we use to describe the individual Christian life. So, the idea that God would walk with us on a beach kind of fits our perception of the relationship we have with Him. However, if we are going to be honest about the life of faith in God, it's not always a "walk." Sometimes we're running to Him, other times we're running away from Him. During the good times, it feels like we're dancing. Other times, it seems like rather than looking back and seeing one set of footprints where God carried us, we actually see a long groove in the sand where He had to drag us kicking and screaming!

As we move forward through this book on the heroes of our faith in **Hebrews 11**, the next person we come to is one about whom we know very little. But the most important thing to know about Enoch is that he "walked faithfully with God" (**Genesis 5:21-24**). The writer of Hebrews includes Enoch in the list of faithful heroes but doesn't tell us about a specific circumstance of faith. Instead, we read these words: "By faith, Enoch was taken from this life, so that he did not experience death" (**Hebrews 11:5**). Did you stop and think about what that means? This man did not die. He was one of two known people (Elijah being the other) to go straight from this life to the next. Why? What would cause such an amazing thing to happen? The answer might surprise you, but it shouldn't.

Back in **Genesis 5:21-24**, we see that Enoch lived 65 years before having his first child, whom he named Methuselah. Let's understand that this took place before the flood during Noah's time that wiped almost everything and everyone off the face of the earth, so that could explain why people lived for so many more years than we do now and also why they had children later in life. The Word doesn't tell us anything about those first 65 years of Enoch's life, but it does tell us that after Methuselah was born, Enoch then walked with God for 300 years before God took him away (**v. 22**). That means we can surmise that the turning point in Enoch's life and his desire to begin to walk with God was the birth of his son.

Now, anyone who has become a parent knows that things change and your child makes you want to be a better person and possibly even a more faithful follower of God. So, on the surface, you may be wondering what the big deal is. But there is more to it than the typical new parent type of change. Enoch lived during a time of great wickedness. Think about the fact that sin and its consequences increased from merely eating a piece of fruit in disobedience to God (Adam and Eve) to one brother murdering another (Cain and Abel) in just ONE generation on this earth. Then think what could happen in seven generations and we get to the time of Enoch. Abel and Enoch are the only two people mentioned as faithful from Adam all the way to Noah, and Abel was murdered way before Enoch came along! The world must have been a pretty lonely place for Enoch if he was the only one alive faithfully walking with the Lord. It would have made so much more sense and been easier for him to just blend in with everyone else and live a wicked life. I guess there had to be a pretty strong motivation for him to walk faithfully with God.

I discovered his motivation when I read a little further in the Bible, researched the meaning of some names, and did some math. If you don't care for research or math, I hope you'll at least get your Bible out and follow this logic because I was blown away by this.

Genesis 7:11 tells us about the great flood that came over the earth when Noah was 600 years old. This is the flood that destroyed everything and everyone on the earth except for those who were in the ark and animals that could fly or live in the water. The rest of the numbers can be found in **Genesis 5:25-31**. Working backwards from the time of Noah, we see that Noah's father was Lamech, and he lived 595 years AFTER Noah was born, which means he died 5 years before the flood. That's easy math so hopefully you're still with me. Then, we are told Lamech lived a total of 777 years. It tells us Lamech's father was Methuselah (who I remind you is the son of

Enoch). We see in these verses that Methuselah lived 782 years AFTER Lamech was born, which means he outlived his son by 5 years. As we already established, Lamech died 5 years before the flood. This means that Methuselah died either IN the great flood or just before it came.

All of this would be irrelevant without one critical piece of information. One translation of the name "Methuselah" is "when he is dead, it shall be sent." In the case of Methuselah, the "it" would be the great flood, which came as God's judgment against the wickedness of mankind. Circling back to the faith of Enoch, you can begin to see why he walked with God AFTER his son was born. There's no doubt in my mind that Enoch received a special revelation from God when his son was born. The revelation showed him that at the end of his son's life, God's judgment would come against the entire world. If you were given that information, you'd probably change how you were living too!

Fear can be the best motivator. Sometimes we soften the idea of "fearing God" in the church. We speak of it as if it's different than other fears because God loves us and we don't need to be afraid that He will destroy us. While it's true that He does love us, it's still just as important as ever to remember that He CAN destroy us completely. Knowing that His judgment could arrive at any moment should motivate us to do everything we can to avoid the ways of the wicked. Methuselah was the oldest person that ever lived. He was 969 years old, yet he died in the exact year of the flood, proving that God does not merely predict things - He PROMISES!

Enoch began walking faithfully with the Lord as soon as his son was born. That tells me that he wasn't given a future timeline. For all he knew, his son would die very young and that would mean everyone else would face judgment as well.

As you read this book, I encourage you to ask yourself if you know how much time you have left on this earth. The answer should be obvious. Given that judgment could come for any of us at any moment, maybe we ought to take it seriously and flee from all types of immorality. Let's continue speaking the truth in love to one another and let's motivate each other to walk faithfully with God for as much time as he gives us!

CHAPTER 4
THE FAITH OF NOAH

There's a joke that goes around in churches that states, "If you want to hear God laugh, tell him about your plans." A movie came out in 2007 with a scene where God actually does laugh at the main character's plans. The movie was called *Evan Almighty* and many of you have probably seen it. Evan Baxter is a politician who just moved from Buffalo to the Washington D.C. area to begin his term as a U.S. Congressman. His plan and his motto state that he is going to "change the world." Then one day, signs start appearing in his life to show him that he may be doing something he hadn't "planned." Eventually, God (played by Morgan Freeman) appears to him a couple times and tells Evan he wants him to build an ark for a flood that will be coming. Evan starts talking about all the plans he had and how he doesn't have time for the ark, and God just starts cracking up. It takes a while, but Evan slowly begins to get the picture that life is only going to get more difficult if he doesn't do what God is commanding him to do.

It's not that God is literally sitting up in heaven laughing at our plans. But the point of the joke is that God doesn't necessarily consider OUR plans, especially the ones we've made without consulting Him, when He asks us to do something big or even just something different. Making plans is not a bad thing. Football teams have a game plan. Those who want to lose weight or get healthier have a workout plan and maybe a diet plan. Businesses have a marketing plan. Couples make wedding plans. You get the picture. But what happens when God allows something to come into your life that you weren't expecting? Is there enough flexibility in your plans and goals that you can consistently follow God by faith when it doesn't seem to line up with the direction you thought you were heading?

Evan Baxter is a fictional character, but he was purposefully created to give us a sense of what it may have been like for Noah in the Bible. Noah is the next hero of our faith in this book where we take a look at the examples of others who went before us and had to put their trust and hope in the Lord even in the midst of difficult or unexpected trials. Let's remember that the foundational verse is **Hebrews 11:3**, where we see that we, like each of the heroes that are then mentioned, actually reason that God created the entire universe out of nothing. Once we've established that foundation, it makes logical sense that He could be trusted to work any miracles that we need as we follow Him. **Hebrews 11:7** then tells us about Noah's faith, which caused him to fear the Lord and build an ark to save his family.

Have you ever thought about what an ark actually is? Because of the story of Noah, it's now mainly defined as the boat that saved people during the worldwide flood. But here's the thing, it wasn't a boat back then! In fact, it still wouldn't really be an accurate definition today because it cannot be steered or sailed. The only thing it can do is float. At the time of Noah, an ark was basically a wooden box or chest used for storage and protection of valuable items. So, when God spoke to Noah in **Genesis 6:13-14a** and told him that He was going to "put an end to all people" because of their wickedness and then commanded Noah to make a wooden ark, he was probably initially very confused. On the one hand, he would've assumed the ark was no different than any other arks that had been made, so he could have it done by that night! On the other hand, he had to be thinking, "Lord, how is a little wooden box going to save me from worldwide catastrophe?" But then God gives him the rest of the command. In **Genesis 6:14b-21**, God tells Noah to "make rooms in it" and then reveals the monstrous dimensions of the ark and also how it will be used during the flood. When I picture Noah hearing this, I sense that he went from thinking, "Piece of cake" to "That's impossible!"

There is no way Noah could have expected what God was going to ask him to do. **Genesis 6:9** tells us that he was righteous and faithful to God, so he may have been spiritually and physically prepared. But it most certainly was not in his plans. Like all of us, he probably had other plans that involved a daily routine and taking care of his family. At best, he was waiting for God to show him how he might fulfill the promise his father made at his birth. **Genesis 5:29** tells us that the name "Noah" sounds like the Hebrew word for "comfort," and his father Lamech said, "He will comfort us in the labor and painful toil of our hands caused by the ground the Lord has cursed." Try living with that pressure. The story of the curse has been passed down from Adam to each generation and you've been told that YOU are the one who will bring comfort. Maybe that's what caused him to walk closer to God.

I'm sure Noah had to spend some time dealing with his feelings about what God commanded, just like Evan Baxter in the movie. Thousands of years later, Jesus would do the same (**Matthew 26:38-42**). We all have those moments when doing what we know God wills seems overwhelming. But, while the Holy Spirit helps us process those feelings, it's ultimately how we respond in action and not how we feel that matters going forward. **Genesis 6:22** tells us, "Noah DID everything just as God commanded him" (caps mine). He followed every detail, and **Hebrews 11:7** says he moved with "holy fear." It also says that by his faith, he condemned the world. Noah wasn't the only one who knew about the coming flood. God didn't tell him to keep it a secret. If you were Noah and you received that kind of information, you'd share it with people. But Noah was the only one who lived by faith. Once the flood came and Noah, his family, and the animals were securely in, **Genesis 7:16** tells us that, "the Lord shut him in." Judgment came for those who didn't believe, whether they planned and were prepared for it or not.

Judgment will come for each of us as well. The fact that God is the one who shut the door and not Noah is one of the most fascinating and commonly overlooked things in the Bible in my opinion. Think about it. Did Noah want people to die? Of course not! He was a righteous and faithful man, so there is no reason to assume he wanted to condemn anyone to death. Chances are he was yelling for people to get on the ark even until the last day! What a burden it would've been on him had he been the one to close the door and keep people out. It also would have been inconsistent with God's character. He alone is faithful and just and He alone judges the whole world. Noah may have been righteous and faithful, but he was not perfect.

Friends, we so often try to condemn people with our words and judgments. If you've ever decided that you think someone is in heaven or hell based on what YOU know about them, that's what you're doing. Maybe God just wants us to shut up and focus on living by faith, and let him be the Judge. Trust and follow Him. You'll be set apart by action from those who don't.

CHAPTER 5
THE FAITH OF ABRAHAM, PART 1

Like many people, I've had seasons of my life when, now that I look back on them, I can see that I was settling. One such time was after I graduated college. I had grown up in Pennsylvania and knew that God was calling me to go to seminary and eventually be a pastor, but that meant moving to a faraway land known as Findlay, Ohio, for a minimum of three years. That was going to be very uncomfortable. I'd have to move away from my family, lose a lot of friendships, and go where I had no network of support and little money. I had been preaching for many years and there was no doubt about my specific calling, but for the first time in my life I would have to seriously walk by faith and trust God. Needless to say, I decided against it.

Those who know my story are thinking, "Wait a minute, I thought he did go to seminary and live in Ohio." It's true that I did, but I'm here to tell you now that I delayed my move quite a bit. Let me just tell you, when God calls you to something and you have no doubt about it whatsoever, never delay! I searched for comfort in relationships with women, in a good-paying job, in friends, in my social life, and in setting up ways to make sure all MY needs were met. But the more I resisted what God was urging me to do, the more I felt uneasy and unsatisfied. It wasn't until a friend and leader in the church called me out on my sin of settling and told me I would continue to lack purpose and passion until I obeyed God that I finally decided to do so. Had I not gone to Ohio, I probably wouldn't be a pastor, wouldn't have met my wife, and wouldn't even know what Worldview Warriors is, let alone be writing for this ministry, including this book!

A man who we know as Abraham, originally named "Abram," was prone to settling at one point in his life. Yet, he learned to obey God and walk faithfully. We will spend three chapters focusing on this man and his journey, as there is much to learn and apply to our own lives. **Hebrews 11** has more to say about him than anyone else.

Our foundational verse of **Hebrews 11:3** certainly applies to him. Abram was given a promise without many specific details, yet he knew that a God who formed the entire universe out of what is not seen could handle the details. That first step is basically where I got hung up before I followed the call. I was worried about all my needs and so many details that God had already figured out since before the world was created! If you've experienced such a time in your life, you can learn from Abraham's faith.

Hebrews 11:8-9 tells us that Abraham "obeyed and went" when God called him to a place where he would receive what was promised "even though he did not know where he was going." We also see that he had to live as a stranger in a foreign land and basically camp in tents. He didn't even have a house for crying out loud! Talk about trusting God for your needs!

To make sure we're all brought up to speed, you can learn about the promise to Abram in **Genesis 12:1-7**. First, he is told to leave his home, his native land, his friends, and even his father's household, but he is not provided with the destination. He is simply told that God will show him a land. God probably knew that Abram wouldn't go just based on that alone and would just chalk it up to bad wine or a weird dream. So, God adds the incentive by promising to make Abram into a great nation and to bless all peoples through him. Let's face it, we're all promised things from time to time. The promise alone is irrelevant unless we believe we can trust the "Promise-r" to fulfill it. Abram had to leave all of those comforts and trust God even though God wouldn't even tell him where he was going. God wasn't forcing him. He could have rejected the call and then went about his business. But he probably would have found, like I and maybe you did, that settling for less than the best God has for you only brings discontentment. Maybe he already knew it.

I find it interesting that when we read this story, we tend to focus on the fact that Abram was not given a destination. We think God is being a little unreasonable with this call and we wonder how we could ever respond the way Abram did. But what if I told you that it's not always about where you're going? Sometimes, it's about WHAT you're leaving behind.

Look again at what God says to Abram in **Genesis 12:1**. God does nothing by coincidence, so you better believe that He wanted to remind Abram of what he needed to leave rather than put his focus on where he was going to end up. Many Biblical scholars believe that Abram's father and his native people were big into idolatry. While we don't know that for certain, I always think about the fact that we read about the faith of Abram but not the faith of his father. In fact, that's true about most of the heroes of our faith. But I have a free piece of advice for you: if you are currently operating in an environment that encourages participation in anything that you know is not acceptable in God's eyes and it is bringing you down rather than bringing you up, I can promise you that God is "calling" you to leave that environment. He wants you to RUN, not walk, away from sin.

Not doing what God commands is sin, and Abram's father showed him how to sin in this manner. **Acts 7:2-3** tells us that the call to head to the land of Canaan came to Abram while he was still in Mesopotamia. Abram's family lived specifically in the land of Ur in that area, and **Genesis 11:31** tells us that his father, Terah, took the family and set out from there to go to the land of Canaan. This was the actual Promised Land that God would give Abram and where Israel is still located to this day. But that same verse shows us that they came to Harran and "settled" there. When Abram followed God in **Genesis 12:4**, he set out from - guess where - Harran! That means it was only after they had settled for less than God's best that Abram chose to follow God as he should have in the first place.

The name "Terah" means "delay." Friends, you may have learned to settle and even been encouraged to settle by your parents or those around you. But God wants so much more for you. He has promises for you. Abram's name, which meant "exalted father," was changed to Abraham, which means "father of many," only after he began to trust God for his basic needs and also that what God promised would all come true.

We'll dig into this more later, but keep in mind that we cannot get what we want in this world by trying to "exalt" ourselves and make sure WE are taken care of. **1 Peter 5:6** tells us that only AFTER we humble ourselves before God will He "lift (us) up in due time." Abram learned the idols of SELF and SETTLING from his father, but he received the promise and the praise from God after he humbly obeyed and trusted Him.

In whatever area you know you are currently settling because you are worried about meeting your own needs, I urge you to trust the God who made everything you see from that which you cannot see. He will not fail you, and He never breaks his promises!

CHAPTER 6
THE FAITH OF ABRAHAM, PART 2

How do you like being told to wait for something you desperately want or need? That's a dumb question, right? I mean, who enjoys waiting? Some of you might be thinking that you don't mind it, but I would guess that means you're just better at dealing with it than most people. Plus, if you think you're a patient person, you've probably never had to wait multiple decades for something promised to you for which you had literally changed your entire life.

The better evaluation than whether or not we like waiting is to think about how we handle it. What do we DO when we are waiting? Do we sit on our hands and do nothing? Do we get frustrated and try to obtain what we're waiting for a different way? Do we just try our hardest to forget about it and settle for less? These responses were all part of the waiting process for Abraham and Sarah.

In the last chapter, we dug into the first part of Abraham's story in the Bible, which took place when he was still known as Abram. We looked at his faith in leaving his family, native country, and everything he knew to go to a place God had not yet even revealed to him, all because that is what God told him to do. However, we also looked at the fact that after he and his family set out with his father to go where God was sending him, they settled in a different town and stayed there for a long time. Abram, like many of us, learned how to settle from his father and needed a little extra motivation to get moving. God promised him great things, but we saw previously that his decision to finally follow God was much more about what he needed to leave than where he was headed. Once he and his wife began the journey of faith, there was no turning back, even though the tests and trials were only beginning.

Hebrews 11:8-12 tells us a little bit about their circumstances. When they were known as Abram and Sarai, they lived in tents in a foreign country and weren't even concerned with having their own home or land because their focus was on the future home and city where they would reside in heaven (**v. 10**). But during that time, they also remembered the promise God gave to Abram, which was that he would be "made into a great nation." He may not have known exactly what this meant yet, but he had a pretty good idea that it had something to do with children. That being said, Abram was 75 years old when he left Harran where he had been settling (**Genesis 12:4**). He had zero children. So, if God was going to make this happen, it was going to need to be really soon!

Our Hebrews passage tells us about BOTH Abraham and Sarah, reminding us that unity is of utmost importance when a married couple is trying to walk in their faith. I'm sure there were times of bickering between them, but it was important that they both be on board with trusting God during their difficult circumstances. Going through hard times is tough enough on its own, but when there is disunity and dysfunction in the family structure, it virtually guarantees your faith won't stand. **Hebrews 11:11-12** tells us that Sarah's faith enabled her to conceive a child long after she was past the age of childbearing, and that allowed Abraham to experience the fulfillment of the promise to become a great nation even though he was "as good as dead."

As it is with all of the heroes of our faith in **Hebrews 11**, the faith of this couple didn't come without some major hiccups. To understand the journey they took, we need to be familiar with more of their story. About ten years after they obeyed God and left Harran, nothing had changed. Could you wait ten years for a promise from God to come to fruition? We read nothing about Abram complaining during that time, but in **Genesis 15:1-8**, God comes out of nowhere and appears to Abram to remind him that HE is Abram's true reward. Abram had to be thinking, "Man, I was doing well with the whole unfulfilled promise thing until you had to go and remind me!" Abram then questions how the promise could come true since he has no children and his servant will get everything he owns, but that's when God reminds him that his descendants will be as numerous as the stars in the sky. In other words, they will be too numerous to count.

At this point, Abram and Sarai do what many of us would do. They get tired of waiting and assume that God needs them to take action in order to accomplish the impossible. This would be a good time for us to be reminded that while God often wants us to take action steps in connection with our faith, He doesn't NEED them. Also, He'll never ask us to do something that contradicts His own Word.

Sarai decided it was her barrenness that was preventing them from having a child, so she concocts a plan to have Abram sleep with her servant, Hagar (**Genesis 16**). Abram figures his wife is not only okay with him sleeping with someone else, but she requests it, so how can he say "no" to that deal? True leadership would have been to refuse to go against God's command and to be patient even when his wife wasn't. Their decision leads to Hagar becoming pregnant, and Abram is 86 years old when his son Ishmael is born. You can read the story for yourself to see the ripple effect of sin and the fact that God does not bless their sinful plan.

Then, another 13 years go by. Could you wait 24 years for a promise God gave you? **Genesis 17** then records the conversation where God again reminds Abram of the promise and changes his name to "Abraham," which means "father of many nations." He challenges Abraham to "walk faithfully and be blameless" in order to receive God's promise (**vv. 1-2**). He then requires Abraham and all the males in his home, as well as all future descendants of Abraham, to be circumcised as the sign of their end of the covenant. After He requires this, He finally, after 24 years, tells Abraham directly that his wife Sarah will become pregnant with the son who will be the heir of the promise "at this time next year" (**v. 21**). In case you had any doubts about Abraham's faith, he then gets circumcised… at NINETY-NINE years old! I don't even want to imagine it, but that's what God said. If we want to receive the blessings of God, we must be willing to do what He says even if we don't like it or it doesn't make sense.

When Abraham hears the specific promise, he laughs, almost directly at God (**Genesis 17:17**). Sarah later does the same thing (**Genesis 18:12**). So God tells them their son's name will be "Isaac," which means "he laughs." If we were in their shoes, we probably would have laughed too. What else can you do after the journey they'd been through? But the most important thing is that despite their frustrations, doubts, sins, and laughter, they chose to again be faithful. When Isaac was born with his dad 100 years old and his mom 90 years old, they gave him the name the Lord commanded. But this time, Sarah and Abraham thanked God for their laughter. Faith allowed them to go from laughing AT God to laughing WITH God (**Genesis 21:6-7**). They overcame their fears and human plans in the midst of waiting and received the promise they thought would never come.

Friends, whatever you're going through, don't give up. God wants to bring you to a point where you can look back on it and LAUGH. Trust Him to take you there.

CHAPTER 7
THE FAITH OF ABRAHAM, PART 3

My wife and I had the pleasure of going on what was, at the time, the trip of our lives for our honeymoon in the summer of 2016. Thanks to the Lord providing for us through several different avenues, we were able to spend an entire week on the island of Kaua'i in Hawaii. While there are some who have the means to take a trip like that every year, we felt it was pretty likely this would be our only chance to visit such a place in our lifetimes. That reality gave me a little bit of a different perspective on the trip. I found that there was a little bit of pressure to try to make sure we saw and experienced everything we could on the island. We rented a Chevy Camaro convertible in order to see and experience it "the right way." As the week continued, I began to grieve the end of it, almost as much as I was thankful for the amazing vacation.

Most of us have had experiences like that. We focus so much on the great gift we are receiving and grasp it so tightly out of fear or sadness of losing it that we forget to remain grateful. The heroes of our faith had to learn to have the opposite view, depending on their God and Creator while everything else around them was falling apart. Abraham and Sarah received a promise from God very early in their journey, but while things did not seem to be going according to plan, their choice was whether to trust in the promise or the Promiser.

In **Hebrews 11:13-16**, we see that Abraham and Sarah got to a point where they were "assured" of the promises made to them even though those promises were still far away. This echoes what we see in **Hebrews 11:1**. Even though they didn't understand why things weren't happening as quickly as they thought, they "embraced" what the Promiser had revealed to them. The Greek word for "embraced" in that passage can also be translated "saluted." The passage gives us the idea that the promises of God were like a constant companion for Abraham and Sarah. Even if they were far away, the couple never let them out of their sight. What if we tried this? Could we wake up each morning while we face difficulties and greet or "salute" God's promises? That intentional acknowledgement could change your life!

For Abraham and Sarah, God's promises caused them to live as "strangers and pilgrims on the earth" (**v. 13**). The passage goes on to tell us that the more they trusted in God and embraced His promises, the more they ignored whatever they left behind. Had they been thinking about what they left, they could have gone back (**v. 15**). When we focus on God instead of all the things we have to leave or all the things we love that come to an end in this life, we can truly begin to see our true home as heaven rather than the temporary attachments we have here.

We're now in our third and final chapter of looking at the faith of Abraham (his wife Sarah was obviously a huge part of the story as well). We've looked at everything they went through and the patience in the midst of trials that God required of them. Because Abraham learned through those situations to depend so much on the Promiser rather than the promise, he was ready for his toughest trial yet.

Hebrews 11:17-19 describes his faith even as he was ready to sacrifice his own son, Isaac, who was to be the heir of the promise Abraham had begun to embrace. Let's remember that God started by promising to make Abraham into a great nation (**Genesis 12:2**), then proceeded to tell him his descendants would be as numerous as the stars in the sky (**Genesis 15:4-5**), then finally guaranteed him that he and his wife would have a son at the ripe old ages of 100 and 90, that they would name him "Isaac," and that he would be the heir to the original promise (**Genesis 17:17-19**). Isaac was born 25 YEARS after the original promise. You'd think that after God made Abraham go through all of that, He'd finally agree to just leave him alone and let him live in peace! Surely, Abraham had passed the test of faith.

We ought to know that God does not do things our way. He doesn't act or think like we presume that He "should," because His ways and thoughts are higher than ours (**Isaiah 55:8-9**). After finally giving Abraham and Sarah the son they were waiting for, God still had more purposes for Abraham as the "father" that many nations would look to as an example of faith. So, He decided to test Abraham once again.

Genesis 22 tells us the story of God appearing to Abraham and commanding him to take Isaac up on a mountain and sacrifice him as a burnt offering. You can read the story on your own, and I strongly encourage you to do so because there is so much to learn and see. There are so many parallels between Isaac in the Old Testament and Jesus in the New Testament, from the fact that Isaac was the "only begotten son" of the promise, to the fact that he trusted his father no matter what, to the geographical region where it took place being a mountain outside of what later became Jerusalem, to the sacrifice being over wood, to the relief coming on the third day, to God himself ultimately providing the lamb for the sacrifice. For the purposes of learning from Abraham's faith, the most important thing for us to know is that he was obedient, and then to understand why.

Genesis 22:3 tells us that Abraham did what God commanded him to do the very next morning after he received the order. **Verse 8** tells us that he was confident in God's ability to provide a lamb for the burnt offering, but **verse 10** tells us that he was also ready to go through with killing his son just before God intervened and stopped him. Why was he willing to kill his son, who was the only one that would be able to carry out the promise God had given him?

Hebrews 11:19 gives us the answer. Abraham "reasoned" that even if he killed his own son, God was able and willing to raise him back to life. Abraham was so confident that whatever God said was true and right, even if it seemed crazy and contrary to everything else. He believed that he couldn't go wrong following the Promiser, who he knew he could trust to come through no matter what. We must not assume that Abraham knew God would stop him, just to make it easier to relate to our own lives. He only knew that God was in control, and he couldn't go wrong with full obedience. May we all learn to simply obey and trust God with the results.

Going back to our foundational verse of **Hebrews 11:3**, I believe that Abraham was able to "reason" that God could raise the dead only because he first understood that God made everything in the universe out of nothing. Faith in God is not blind; it makes the most sense. As of Abraham's time, no one had ever been raised from the dead. But if our foundation of faith is that God made everything from nothing, then is there anything He can't do? Regardless of what God requires of you in this life, always ask yourself if you truly have any reason to doubt Him. He might ask you to give up more than you ever thought you could, but obedience will never go wrong for you. When everything else will fade away, He is the one sure thing.

CHAPTER 8
THE FAITH OF ISAAC

Before you do anything else today, grab the closest box to you. Does it look like a box that could contain the living God? That might seem like a silly question, but human beings often try to put their Creator in a figurative "box," as if He ought to bless our plans and our will rather than us serving Him.

To further illustrate how foolish this is, you may be familiar with the photo of the "pale blue dot." The photo was taken by the Voyager 1 spacecraft in 1990 from a record distance of 3.7 billion miles from earth. Oh, and by the way, that pale blue dot in that photo IS planet earth. The Bible tells us that God created all of that and some other stuff in one day. Then on a separate day, God created the sun, moon, and stars.

I was reminded of God's greatness once when I was awoken in the middle of the night by my wife's cat and decided to go outside and try to see a meteor shower that was advertised. While I did see 3 meteors that night, I couldn't help but be amazed by the things that are in the sky EVERY night - the stars. I looked up and saw more stars than I could count, yet I remember that the Bible says, "He also made the stars," like they were an afterthought for God in the midst of everything else he was creating (**Genesis 1:16**).

God is so much bigger than our finite minds can even possibly comprehend, yet we try to fit Him into OUR plans. Maybe you are still begging Him to bless the dysfunctional relationship you're in rather than patiently waiting for Him to bring you the right person. Maybe you want God to take away your desires for drugs, alcohol, or pornography but you still want to be able to "dabble" in them from time to time. Maybe you are asking God to bless you financially, but you aren't willing to work hard for it or to give God what He commands from your income. If any of these circumstances describe your life currently, you can learn from Isaac's example.

In **Hebrews 11:20**, all we see about Isaac is that his faith caused him to "bless Jacob and Esau in regard to their future." That may seem insignificant until you learn that the Greek word for "blessed" there is "eulogeo," which simply means "to praise." It's also where we get the English word "eulogy." One of the most important parts of a funeral is the eulogy, a time when the deceased person is praised and remembered for their characteristics, achievements, or faith. As a society, we generally only eulogize someone after they have passed. Yet, Isaac had faith in a God who was bigger than his plans and his view of the future and chose to eulogize them regarding what God determined would happen. Going back to our foundational verse of **Hebrews 11:3**, Isaac knew that if God could create everything in the universe out of what is not seen, then He can certainly be trusted with the future.

Just like his mother and father, Sarah and Abraham, Isaac did not have perfect faith that was without struggle. However, he started out on the right track. In the story we talked about in the last chapter from **Genesis 22**, where Isaac was about to be sacrificed according to God's command to Abraham, Isaac was completely submissive and trusting toward his father. Let's not forget that Abraham was well over 100 years old and Isaac was a young man, easily the stronger of the two. Had he wanted to overpower his elderly father, he could have.

But Isaac was a foreshadowing of Jesus, who humbled himself as a man and became obedient to a horrible death (**Philippians 2:5-8**). That is the only way God can be put into a box - when He chooses to put Himself in it temporarily! Isaac trusted his father, and we see the same thing happen again in **Genesis 24** when Isaac does not try to find a partner on his own, but he waits on the Lord to provide his future wife through the efforts of his father and a servant. Isaac could've doubted God, as he knew he was the heir of the promise yet did not yet have a wife who might bear him a son. But his faith was still intact, and God blessed him with Rebekah.

When you are walking with God and putting your faith and trust in him, Satan just leaves you alone, right? NOT! **Genesis 25** brings us the death of Abraham, followed by some of the same struggles for

Isaac and Rebekah that Abraham and Sarah faced. Isaac and Rebekah deal with infertility and pray to the Lord about it. When we have questions about his promises, we are always invited to go straight to him. He's not afraid to be questioned. Rebekah is then told she will have twin sons, one who will be stronger than the other. Just like with Isaac and Ishmael as sons of Abraham, one child represents life with God and the other life without God.

Isaac's two sons are Jacob and Esau, and even though God had revealed that the promise would continue through Jacob, **verse 28** tells us that Isaac favors Esau over Jacob because Esau is a skilled hunter and Isaac loves the wild game. Because Rebekah favors Jacob more, this was the start of the family dysfunction and slow fade away from faith that would mark a large part of the rest of their story.

In **Genesis 26**, we see that even after God reminds Isaac of the promise and is very clear about what he should do, Isaac lies about his wife Rebekah to a foreign king, much in the same way that Abraham had lied about Sarah. In both cases, the men of God chose to live by sight rather than faith. They allowed their own plans and fears to overcome their faith momentarily, and God's plan and promise are threatened by the very clear plans of the devil. Read the chapter and see for yourself how God thwarts the devil's schemes despite Isaac not living by faith.

While God's plan cannot be destroyed by sin, we certainly experience the consequences of it. At the very end in **verses 34-35**, we see that Isaac's favorite son, Esau, marries two pagan women that become a source of grief for his parents. This comes as no surprise because Esau had disregarded his spiritual blessing, referred to back then as his "birthright," a long time before this.

You can read **Genesis 27** to see how the family dysfunction really takes on a whole new level. It's the stuff you'd see on a daytime talk show. I'm talking about lies, distrust, gossip, eavesdropping, and deception. God has made it clear which son gets the blessing and which son has chosen to go his own way and marry pagan women and disregard the blessing that would have originally been his, yet Isaac still favors Esau based solely on "manly" characteristics. He tries to bless Esau, but Rebekah and Jacob deceive him into blessing Jacob. It isn't until after all this happens that Isaac basically says, "You win, God." In **verse 33**, he states that Jacob will "indeed be blessed." Despite all of Isaac's efforts otherwise, Jacob received the blessing, and it was as if Isaac finally accepted this was God's will. His final blessing to Jacob in **Genesis 28:1-4** shows that Isaac is finally on board with God's will and choosing to live by faith.

While the Hebrew birthright takes on a cultural significance that we might not fully grasp in our society, it was connected to the original promise to Abraham and all future Israelites because of this family. Isaac initially tried to box God's will into his own plans but later came to accept what God wanted by faith. That faith allowed him to see the future through God's eyes rather than his own, which led to complete trust and a proper "eulogy" for his sons.

If you have an area of your life where you have not been trusting the Lord and you've been in the same vicious and dysfunctional cycle of begging Him to bless the plans you have already made, it's time to realize that you can only find true happiness and fulfillment in letting HIM set your course and walking accordingly.

Chapter 9
The Faith of Jacob

Have you ever taken on something in your life that you knew right away you had absolutely no clue how to manage? For my wife Clara and me, that thought described just about everything in our lives in 2017. After leaving friends, jobs, and comfort in Ohio and moving to Pennsylvania, we purchased a house for the first time in our lives, and then discovered soon after that we were going to be parents! While the general response we had gotten from all of our friends and family had been congratulatory and celebratory - and rightfully so since all of these things are blessings from the Lord - we'd be lying if we denied that there had at least been some angst as we approached each of these undertakings. I had never been a full-time pastor until then, my wife had never been an executive director of a faith-based agency that relies heavily on donations until then, and neither of us had ever owned a home or been a parent. But whether we were ready or not, all those things became simultaneous realities in 2018.

Obviously, we have had at least some control and choice in each of these things. Not a single one of them has "happened" to us. They are things we want and things for which we believe God has been preparing us. But the simple fact that we have so many unknowns and the pressure to "not mess it up" had caused us to have some fear. Now, there are probably more times that we feel confident and have hope.

I got to wondering about the difference between the two feelings for us - fear versus hope. What I realized is that the times we start worrying about things and losing sight of the true blessings we are receiving are when we are too focused on US, and the times we feel content, secure, confident, and hopeful are when we accept and even laugh about the fact that we have no clue about most of this stuff and are fully dependent on GOD working His good plans in and through us.

What I have described here for all of us is the universal battle of our flesh versus God's will. The man we'll look at in this chapter certainly had his struggles between his carnal view and seeing things through God's eyes. But like most of the other heroes of the faith, his struggles were merely speed bumps on his road to confident faith.

Hebrews 11:21 tells us about Jacob's faith that guided him to the very end: "By faith Jacob, when he was dying, blessed each of Joseph's sons, and worshiped as he leaned on the top of his staff." Jacob is discussed in basically half of the chapters in the book of Genesis, so it's interesting that the writer of Hebrews only mentions his faith at the very end as the example to us. So, let's go back and check a little bit of Jacob's history.

As we saw in the last chapter, Bible readers first meet Jacob in **Genesis 25** when the story of the births of him and his twin Esau are detailed. Because of how he is grabbing Esau's heel when he is born, he is named "Jacob" by his mother, which means "he grasps the heel" and is a Hebrew idiom for "one who deceives" (**verse 26**). This tells us right away that Jacob will be one who manipulates and deceives in order to get what he wants or feels he deserves. Jacob eventually cons his brother Esau into giving up his birthright (which Esau would have been due since he was technically the older brother), and this causes Esau to want revenge, so he plans to eventually kill Jacob (**Genesis 27:41**). Jacob knows this and fears his brother's revenge, so he runs away and ends up basically building a life somewhere else. As he goes on his journey, God appears to him in the story where we read about his dream of a stairway to heaven (**Genesis 28:10-22**). If you read those verses, you see that Jacob completely understands that he is not God. He trusts God's promises, sets up a pillar to worship and remember that everything belongs to God, and he makes a vow to obey God with a tithe for as long as God continues to bless him and keep His promises.

If you've read the previous chapters about Abraham and Isaac, you know that there is a pattern with these guys. They start out as faithful, then circumstances, fears, or temptations cause them to act based on their flesh, then they return to their faith in the end. This should be a comfort to us no matter what part of that story we are currently experiencing.

Like Abraham did at the beginning of his story, Jacob settles somewhere that is not ultimately God's plan for him. He ends up marrying two different women (the first time that we know of that someone included in the heroes of our faith committed the sin of polygamy) and sleeps with two other women in addition to his wives. All four of the women bear him children, but the issues of jealousy, insecurity, and family dysfunction reveal that this was NOT God's plan and everyone involved is suffering the consequences of not walking with Him. Yet, after all that, God tells him again that He will be with Jacob if he obeys and goes back to where God wants him (**Genesis 31:3**). Jacob begins to see the truth and refers to God as "the Fear of his father Isaac" (**Genesis 31:53**). He's starting to see that doing things God's way and focusing on God's command rather than his own view works out best!

After Jacob physically struggles between his flesh and God in **Genesis 32** (a physical picture of the spiritual struggle we all have), Jacob's name is changed to "Israel," which means "struggles with God." Of course, God could choose to overpower Jacob's flesh easily, but that's not who God is. Our flesh has to be surrendered, not taken by force. Jacob reconciles with Esau in the next few chapters, then goes through some awful stuff after that, including dealing with the rape of his daughter and two of his sons, then killing the rapist and many others with him out of revenge. While his sons view the situation out of their own flesh, Jacob begins to see things God's way and does not condone the revenge killings. Later, his firstborn son, Reuben, sleeps with Jacob's concubine (**Genesis 35:22**), and Jacob hears about it. Then, his favorite son, Joseph, is taken away by his jealous brothers and is sold into slavery (**Genesis 37**). Jacob is told Joseph is dead and believes it, so he mourns a death that isn't even true for the next 20 years!

When Jacob learns that Joseph is still alive in Egypt many years later, he travels there to see him and trusts God after God tells him to go and not be afraid. While there, he reveals to Joseph that God had promised to make him into a great nation and makes Joseph swear an oath to him that he will carry Jacob's body back to the

Promised Land and bury him next to his father and grandfather. As Joseph swears the oath, **Genesis 47:31** tells us that Jacob leans on the top of his staff. This may seem insignificant, but it's a great example of faith just like the others in **Hebrews 11**.

I remember hearing once that the staff had the carvings of reminders of the great works God had done so far in Israel's history. Jacob was old, weak, and physically handicapped from the dislocation of his hip during his physical struggle with God. Thus, his decision to lean on the staff was an admission that, though he was weak and broken, his dependence would be on God's promises and not his own physical flesh. The same is true in **Genesis 48**, when Jacob reckons Joseph's sons Ephraim and Manasseh as his own and blesses them along with his other ten sons (minus Reuben and Simeon who lost their blessings because of their sins). Even when Joseph is still acting in the flesh and tries to force Jacob to bless his sons as tradition says rather than as God says, Jacob simply does God's will and ignores any tradition that would set itself up against God's plan.

Friends, you may be weak, you may be broken, or you may even be physically handicapped. You may have spent many years away from God or simply went back and forth from following Him to disobeying Him. You may still be wrestling with God and trying to depend on your flesh more than Him even now. Regardless of what place you are at in your journey, you can learn from Jacob's example that it's not too late to surrender to the Lord and depend on His will for the things in life that bring you angst, rather than trying to keep control in your own hands. You'll never be more free and at peace than when you accept that you need God to save you from yourself!

Chapter 10
The Faith of Joseph

In the United States, we hold an annual observance called Veterans' Day for those who have served our nation in military service. It reminds us that we have much for which to be thankful in this country and much that we so often take for granted. The service and sacrifice of so many in our military remind us of our Savior, who gave up His very life for not just our nation but the sins of the whole world.

A word that might most accurately describe our veterans' service is "legacy." They love their country and want to be remembered as having contributed to maintaining the freedoms it provides. One man who couldn't bear the thought of his legacy not including some sacrifice or contribution to preserving those freedoms was former NFL player Pat Tillman. He is known for having given up his comfortable life as a professional athlete to join his brother in the Army Rangers during our national conflicts with Iraq and Afghanistan. While anyone who has heard of his story knows that Tillman lost his life in Afghanistan in 2004, many have continued to wonder why he would give up the life that so many would want. The answer can be found in an interview he did the day after September 11, 2001. Tillman mentioned all of his family members who had proudly served their country, then considered that he, by comparison, hadn't done a thing. He would eventually come to the conclusion that a legacy of service and self-sacrifice was better than a legacy of athletic success and lavish living.

How we live, and for that matter how we handle the fact that our lives are but a fraction of God's whole story in the world, says everything about the legacy that remains long after our time. Our hero of the faith for this chapter is Joseph, and he certainly left a lasting legacy of faith and dependence on God.

Hebrews 11:22 tells us, "By faith Joseph, when his end was near, spoke about the exodus of the Israelites from Egypt and gave instructions concerning the burial of his bones." This verse shows us that Joseph had an opportunity to do what many don't, and that's give direct instructions to those who will carry on his legacy just before he dies. Let's go back to the Old Testament and take a look at his story.

Genesis 37:3 tells us that Joseph was loved by Jacob more than any of his brothers. This caused his brothers to hate him. Frankly, Joseph doesn't appear to be that bothered by this, because he dreams that his brothers and his parents will all eventually bow down to him and has no problem sharing these dreams with his family. It's quite possible that Joseph knew how favored he was, and that this led to some level of arrogance.

Later in **Genesis 37:18-36**, we see that his brothers plot to kill him, but instead come up with a better plan to sell him into slavery to a group of foreign merchants, who in turn take him to Egypt and sell him to a man named Potiphar, who was a high-ranking official in Pharaoh's administration. Joseph then spends at least the next 11 years in the home of Potiphar, and although God has allowed terrible and unfair things to happen to him, he lives a life of obedience. When Potiphar's wife tries to sleep with him, he refuses because such an action would be a sin against God (**Genesis 39:6-10**). Unable to deal with his rejection, Potiphar's wife ultimately tries to force him and when even that doesn't work, she accuses him of attempted rape. That's a death sentence in that time and culture, given that she was the wife of a high-ranking government official.

But God continues to work in Joseph's life as Joseph continues to be obedient and faithful despite his circumstances. He is put in prison, but just so we're clear, it's nothing like the prisons we have in America today. **Psalm 105:18** tells us that Joseph's "feet were bruised with shackles and his neck was put in irons." Despite this discomfort, **Genesis 39:21-22** tells us that God gave Joseph favor in the eyes of the prison warden, who then put Joseph in charge of the business and the people in the prison. Joseph didn't know it yet, but God was preparing him for a time in his future when he would use his experience and leadership to save others.

After a few more years in prison and some other unfortunate and unfair happenings, Joseph has an opportunity to interpret dreams for Pharaoh himself. When he does it, Pharaoh puts him in charge of all of Egypt (**Genesis 41:41**). During his service to Pharaoh, Joseph plans ahead and stores up grain during 7 years of abundance because God reveals to him that 7 years of famine are coming after that. When the famine happens, Joseph is able to feed and save people who did not prepare for it.

The group of people saved includes his family. Jacob hears of grain in Egypt and sends Joseph's brothers there to buy some. Joseph recognizes his brothers and after a while chooses to reveal himself to them (**Genesis 45**). This is his best opportunity to really hammer them for what they did to him years earlier, but Joseph's faith and obedience to God are shown in his unwillingness to get them back. He thinks only about how he can help them.

At the end of Jacob's life, Joseph's brothers fear his revenge. But Joseph directly tells them that even though they meant to harm him, "God intended it for good to accomplish what is now being done, the saving of many lives" (**Genesis 50:20**). That kind of perspective on God's work in everything reveals that Joseph trusted God with even his suffering, knowing that a God who created the universe out of nothing (**Hebrews 11:3**) could handle his trials and any necessary vengeance.

It comes as no surprise, then, that Joseph kept that faith in God's great plan in the midst of suffering, even to his last breath and actually beyond it. He could think of nothing better to pass on to his brothers and future Israelite generations than a trust that God would do as He had always promised. In **Genesis 50:24-25**, he tells them that God will "surely" take them out of Egypt and back to the land he had promised to their forefathers. He then makes them swear an oath that they will not bury him where he dies in Egypt, but they will instead take his bones with them WHEN (not "if") they go back to the Promised Land.

Things would get much worse for the Israelites in **Exodus 1** when a new king (aka "another Pharaoh") who couldn't care less about Joseph takes over. It would be 400 years until Joseph's prophecy is fulfilled and Moses does as Joseph asked (**Exodus 13:19**). Yet, all throughout those 400 years, Joseph's body and bones remained in a coffin above the ground, so that anyone who walked by and wondered about it could be reminded that God is still in control and still working in the midst of their circumstances, no matter how bleak they appear.

As things seem to be spinning further and further out of control in our country and around the world today, what legacy are you leaving for your children and those who come after you? Is it one of fear and a need for security? Or are you leaving a legacy of faith and freedom in the knowledge that God is at work and will SURELY do as He promises? If you haven't done it yet, let go and trust God!

CHAPTER 11
THE FAITH OF MOSES' PARENTS, PART 1

In our present culture, there is a lot of attention, discussion, and even outrage toward people, programs, institutions, and belief systems that are deemed to be "oppressive" to certain groups of people. Depending on what particular issue is being addressed, we occasionally find ourselves involved in something where people on BOTH sides feel they are being oppressed. Christians often find themselves in the middle because they want to stay true to God's Word but also don't want to appear as hateful or ungracious. Since those words are generally thrown around anytime someone doesn't like the view of another, it's a realistic concern for believers.

During confusing and frustrating times, we can always find hope in Scripture. The Bible is clear that showing care and concern for the oppressed is not a suggestion; it's a command. In **Isaiah 1**, God is speaking to the Israelites through the prophet and is telling them that they are disobedient and rebellious, just to name two of the adjectives listed there. But in **verse 17**, He specifically tells them to "seek justice" and "defend the oppressed." He then gives more specific information about who is oppressed: "Take up the cause of the fatherless; plead the case of the widow." In other words, those who are most oppressed, according to God's Word, are not those who have had their feelings hurt or who are struggling to deal with the unfairness they have experienced in life. The truly oppressed are those most vulnerable who cannot care for their own needs: widows and orphans.

We should ask ourselves now if anything has changed. Yes, single women and even widows have many more opportunities to provide for their needs in our society than they ever did in Biblical times. But as believers, we ought to pay attention to those who are most vulnerable and dependent on others. Single mothers might be hard-working and almost heroic in the way they juggle all their responsibilities, but they are still at a disadvantage. Widows who have given their whole lives to supporting their husbands or families and now must find a way to function in life with diminished skill sets (at least in the eyes of the working world) need our help. Children who are either unwanted or whose parents can no longer care for them or have passed on are completely dependent on others to meet their basic needs. I believe God will hold us accountable just as He did Israel if we ignore these needs right in front of us.

While many don't want to hear what I'm about to declare, it's something the church in America MUST address. By far, the most oppressed group of human beings in this country and across the planet is unborn children. Some will say it's a controversial statement, but the statistics are indisputable. By anyone's count, over 50 million babies have been aborted in the United States and over 45 million are aborted every year across the world. The vast majority of these babies are simply "orphans," children who God allowed to be created yet remain unwanted by their parents. Even those who may have been wanted at some point had their lives and futures snuffed out in favor of something that took greater priority. Some will say we shouldn't talk about political issues in regard to our faith. Well, good thing it's an issue of faith and not one of politics. By the way, this great sin of oppression has been taking place for thousands of years.

For the next two chapters, our heroes of the faith from **Hebrews 11** are two people that the writer of Hebrews doesn't even mention by name (**Exodus 6:20** tells us they are Amram and Jochebed), but their faith and appreciation for created life stood out during a time when no one would have blamed them for caving to the laws and pressures around them. They were the parents of Moses, a man whom God had planned to lead the Israelites out of captive Egypt since before he was even born. But he faced an instant and very real threat to his life the very moment he opened his eyes for the first time in this world. To understand it, we have to know the history.

In the previous chapter, we talked about the faith of Joseph and his prophecy that the Israelites would surely leave Egypt and his bones would be carried back to the Promised Land. At the time Joseph died, things were good between Pharaoh (king of Egypt), Joseph, and the rest of the Israelites. One reason for this was that the Israelites posed no threat whatsoever to the Egyptians at that point.

But as we transition from Joseph to the Exodus, we learn that circumstances changed. **Exodus 1:6-10** tells us that after Joseph and his family members died, the Israelites experienced their own "baby boomer" era and the land became so full of them that a new Pharaoh who couldn't possibly have cared less about Joseph decided the Egyptians had to do something about them before they join Egypt's enemies and fight against them. **Exodus 1:11-14** shows us that his initial plan was to simply oppress them with ruthless physical labor. He must have assumed that this might control the population a bit.

When that doesn't work and the Israelites only increase (I'll say more about this in the next chapter), in essence Pharaoh resorts to partial-birth abortions, ordering the Hebrew midwives to kill any Hebrew babies that are determined to be males when the mothers are already on the delivery stool (**v. 16**). When that plan doesn't work because the midwives obey God over Pharaoh (I'll say more about this in the next chapter as well), Pharaoh goes a step further and resorts to infanticide, ordering that every Hebrew male baby be thrown into the Nile River (**v. 22**).

This is the setting for Moses' parents to take their great step of faith. When Moses is born, and **Exodus 2:2** tells us that his mother saw he "was a fine child," his parents had a life-changing decision to make. Would they disobey the king's order and risk not only the destruction of their child but also their very lives? Or would they disobey God out of fear of man? Well, **Hebrews 11:23** reminds us of what the next part of **Exodus 2** details, that Moses' parents had faith and demonstrated it by hiding him for three months. They feared God more than the king's heinous order. I suppose that they determined that a God who created the whole universe out of what we can't see (**Hebrews 11:3**) could be trusted to handle life and death concerns.

The story didn't end after those three months. Moses' parents continued to take steps of faith and were ultimately rewarded in a way that only God could truly organize. But for us, we must determine if we trust God enough to accept that He oversees life and death entirely. The alternative is that we succumb to the prevailing worldview of our culture that WE should have ultimate choice in this area. There have been well-known Christian leaders coming down on both sides, as well as others that just try to avoid the issue altogether. But let us all be challenged to do as God commands and look after those who are most vulnerable and oppressed, especially the unborn! I remind you, it's not a suggestion.

Chapter 12
The Faith of Moses' Parents, Part 2

Years ago, I heard about the amazing story surrounding the birth of Tim Tebow, who is known for his athletic achievements at the University of Florida, in the NFL, and as he moved up the minor league system for baseball's New York Mets. However, he is well-known beyond his sports accomplishments, as he is perhaps the most outspoken of any Christian professional athlete in recent memory. Tebow has faced overwhelming support and also harsh criticism for his public displays of faith. He goes on speaking tours and shares the gospel message, has written multiple books, and started the Tim Tebow Foundation, which does a lot of charitable work and events including "Night to Shine," a celebration specifically designed to provide a prom-like experience for teenagers with special needs. The work of Tim Tebow and those who partner with him has touched millions of lives.

If Tim's parents had followed the recommendation of doctors in the Philippines 30 years ago, he would have never seen this world. Tim's mother, Pam Tebow, had complications very early in her pregnancy. The Tebow family was doing missionary work in the Philippines and Pam contracted amoebic dysentery, which is common in places where there is a lack of clean water. Not knowing she was pregnant, doctors prescribed Pam strong antibiotics and she took them. When she later found out she was pregnant, the medication was stopped, but doctors told her that her fetus had already been severely damaged by the medication. When she then began to bleed early in her pregnancy, doctors told her she should abort the baby so that her own life would not be at risk. They even tried to justify their recommendation by convincing her that it wasn't actually a life, but a mass of tissue similar to a tumor. It was only because of their faith in God and his plan that Mr. and Mrs. Tebow chose to trust Him and go forward with the birth, believing that God had a purpose for the life he allowed to be created. Tim was born after having only a very tiny portion of the placenta attached for most of the pregnancy, so the doctors described him as a "miracle baby."

As Pam and Tim Tebow have both traveled the country telling their story, some 5 million women have chosen not to kill their babies after hearing it. Sometimes, we have to overcome fear, anxiety, or even physical pain to experience the blessing that God intends. If we thought Tim Tebow's entrance into the world was a difficult situation, we'll see that it doesn't even compare to the birth of Moses, recorded in **Exodus 2:1-10**.

His birth comes on the heels of Pharaoh's attempts to "deal shrewdly" (**Exodus 1:10**) with the Israelites to keep them from becoming a threat by joining with Egypt's other enemies. He had a good plan, according to a worldly view. First, he oppressed them with hard labor. When that didn't work, he moved forward with partial-birth abortions, and then ultimately, infanticide.

Being "shrewd" isn't always a bad thing. Jesus even tells his disciples in **Matthew 10:16** to be "as shrewd as snakes and innocent as doves" when He is sending them out for ministry. But we must know there is a big difference between being shrewd within God's will and being shrewd AGAINST God's will. The former uses what God created within us, while the latter exposes the folly of those who ignore or even completely reject the presence of the Creator in their lives.

Pharaoh thought he had control over the Israelites by ordering that all Hebrew male babies be thrown into the Nile River (**Exodus 1:22**), but God's plan would not be foiled. When Pharaoh first tried to oppress the people, **Exodus 1:12** tells us, "The more they were oppressed, the more they multiplied and spread." This became the mark of God's people all throughout history. The Church grew the most in the first few centuries after Christ was crucified, when Christians faced some of the most intense persecution of all time. Even today, Christianity is growing fastest in nations in Asia and Africa where persecution is the strongest, while it's declining in America and Europe where believers are most comfortable. As the ancient Christian writer Tertullian said, "The blood of the martyrs is the seed of the church." We must never shy away from persecution or hardships because God may just be using it to grow our faith and testify to others.

After Pharaoh's first plan didn't work, he ordered the Hebrew midwives to kill the babies if they are male while the mothers are in the process of delivering, but the midwives disobeyed his orders and justified it by saying that the Hebrew women are more vigorous and give birth before they arrive (**Exodus 1:19**). This is a perfect example of being shrewd within God's will. They likely did not lie. What is one thing that might cause pregnant women to become more "vigorous"? I'd say hard and oppressive labor would do the trick!

So then Pharaoh gives the command to kill babies that are already alive. In America, we think that's a heinous act and equate it to murder, while at the same time allowing unborn babies to be torn apart. Friends, if we don't continue to stand up and do whatever we can to eradicate the evil that is abortion, don't be surprised if we someday get to the point where we are finding justifications for killing LIVING children that are getting in the way of OUR plans. There is no limit to the depravity of man.

Moses' parents did not fear Pharaoh's order (**Hebrews 11:23**), but trusted by faith that God had a plan for their beautiful son no matter what would happen to them. **Exodus 2:1-10** reveals that Moses' mother decided to place him in a "papyrus basket" (the King James version calls it an "ark," so think about that for a moment and study it if you have the time) and put him into the Nile when he was three months old and they could not hide him any longer. Once again, we see an example of shrewdness that is WITHIN God's plan. Technically, she didn't break Pharaoh's order because she did place the boy in the Nile. Nevertheless, she had to let go of her treasured son and trust God. You parents out there know what it's like to spiritually give your children over to the Lord, but try doing that literally and physically! It's hard for us to even fathom this level of faith.

As it turned out, God's plan was to reward Moses' parents beyond what they could possibly imagine. Pharaoh's daughter discovers the baby floating down the river and has sympathy for him. When she realizes it's a Hebrew baby, Pharaoh has the baby's OWN MOTHER brought to his daughter so that she could nurse the baby and raise him until he was older. On top of that, Pharaoh's daughter even pays Moses' mother to raise him! When he was older, he became Pharaoh's daughter's son, putting him in position to rule in Egypt and eventually lead his people out of their oppression and captivity.

We couldn't make up a better story if we tried! Sure, there will always be people devaluing life and rejecting God's intended plans. It may seem like we have no way out. But God gives us the ability to be innocent and shrewd at the same time. As long as we are acting within His will and honoring Him as Savior, Lord, and Creator, we can wait with confidence and anticipation of the deliverance that we know is coming. Let your faith be your hope and your evidence of all that God will do for those who trust Him!

Moses and the Burning Bush / *Exodus 3:5*
"The place where you are standing is holy ground"

CHAPTER 13
THE FAITH OF MOSES

My family was blessed with an absolutely amazing dog when I was growing up. T.J. was an English springer spaniel who rarely disobeyed us and was always excited to see us. We loved him like a human being and almost always took him with us when we went on trips. One such trip was to a vast wilderness area in northern Pennsylvania known as the Allegheny National Forest. My dad had been to a hunting camp there as a kid and the area is also known for its elk population, so we longed to see the area and hopefully come across some wildlife.

While we were on a hike with T.J., he took off following a scent from some other animal (probably a deer or elk), and the next thing we knew was that he was gone. He stopped listening to us as he followed the scent and took off running, deep into the forest. Suddenly, we all feared the worst, that we would never see him again and some bigger animal would get to him. We did what we could do, which included a foot search and yelling his name for about an hour straight. Despite our efforts, we all knew that we had no control over this situation and were completely dependent on God to watch over T.J. and bring him back to us. If God didn't come through, all hope would have been lost.

I'm happy to say that God did bring T.J. back to us. He eventually came running back to our shouting voices like it was never in doubt. Still, that ordeal was one of my earliest recollections of being in a situation where I knew even my father, who always seemingly had everything under control, was fully dependent on God. As I've gotten older, I've noticed how seldom I, like many other Christians, am comfortable depending on God. It's like we know how to talk about what it means to have faith, but don't ask us to *actually* depend on God with no contingency plan.

After looking at the faith of Moses' parents over the past two chapters, we now look at the faith of their son. Moses' very birth and life had already been works of the Lord that no one could deny, but as he got older he had to learn full dependence on the Lord for himself. Certainly, he was able to reason that if God could create the whole universe out of nothing, he could be trusted above all else (**Hebrews 11:3**). But that reasoning didn't come right away for Moses. He first learns of God's call on his life through the "burning bush" encounter in **Exodus 3**. He was told that God was going to use him to lead his people, the Israelites, out of captivity in Egypt. Moses had been raised in Egypt and had been very close to Pharaoh and his family, so he understandably has a lot of questions, followed by a lot of excuses and complaints (**Exodus 3-4**). The Lord answers every single one, and Moses, now out of stall options, returns to Egypt.

A seemingly shocking incident takes place while Moses is on his way and almost ends the whole thing before it even gets started. **Exodus 4:24-25** tells us that the Lord is about ready to kill Moses until his wife pulls out a knife and immediately circumcises their son. This might seem harsh coming from a loving God, but we have to understand that circumcision was the specific act that God required of all Israelite males to demonstrate their faith and trust in Him. For Moses to either be uncircumcised himself or allow one of his children to go forward uncircumcised was a sin of omission. It was indicative of the guilty party not taking the commands of God seriously. While God had big plans for Moses to lead the people out of Egypt, we must see this story as a reminder that our calling is never bigger than obeying God's commands.

God will not accept disobedience, and as important as Moses was to the big story of God's plan for His people, their rescue from captivity would have gone on without him if he didn't choose to obey God. Moses might have thought the particular command regarding circumcision was of no real consequence so God wouldn't really care. But God taught him that no sin can be ignored just because we don't see the point. God was getting ready to deal with the sins of Pharaoh and all of Egypt, so how could He ignore Moses' sins? It would be out of God's character to do so.

This may have been the turning point for Moses. After that encounter, he meets with his brother Aaron and they go straight to

Pharaoh and ask him to let their people go as the Lord commanded. No matter how insane of an idea that seemed to be, Moses had learned that God was in complete control and he wasn't about to disobey His commands again.

Hebrews 11:24-28 lists several examples of faith from the Exodus story for which Moses was commended. First is his willingness to align himself with the captive Israelites, his true native people, when he could have continued to be known as Pharaoh's grandson and received all the benefits that came with it. We are reminded that this decision meant that he would suffer with them and understood that "disgrace for the sake of Christ was of greater value than the treasures of Egypt, because he was looking ahead to his reward" (**v. 26**). His faith in his eternal prize allowed him to willingly give up the pleasures of sin in Egypt.

Secondly, he and the Israelites left Egypt when God presented the opportunity after a series of devastating plagues rained down on the Egyptians, even though he likely knew that Pharaoh and his vast army would pursue them. **Hebrews 11:27** tells us he was able to do this because he "saw him who was invisible." Pharaoh had all the worldly power, but Moses knew that it didn't compare to the power of God who was fighting their battle for them.

Thirdly, we're told that Moses faithfully kept the Passover and the application of blood. Considering where Moses came from when he began his journey of faith by nearly getting killed for not obeying the seemingly odd command of circumcision, the application of the blood during Passover might be the best example of his faith. In the midst of the craziness of the plagues and all the back-and-forth between Moses and Aaron, God, and Pharaoh, Moses receives what seems like absolutely ridiculous instructions. To this day, Israelites still commemorate Passover as their re-birth as a nation, but think about what it was like to be the first one to hear about the idea.

In **Exodus 12:1-11**, Moses is given all the specific instructions regarding the Passover lamb and how it should be chosen, prepared, and eaten. That may or may not have been weird. But right in the middle of it, he is told they have to take some of the blood from the lamb and wipe it on their doorframes of their houses. Um... huh? Someone with a normal background may have been alarmed, but not Moses. He has already learned his lesson. So, from here on out, all instructions from the Lord, no matter how silly or insane they sound, will be followed without fail. Circumcise everyone? No problem, Lord. Play in the lamb's blood and wipe it on our beloved homes? You got it! Because Moses and the people didn't mess around and followed all of those weird instructions, they were spared during the final plague. Moses' faith and willingness to depend fully on the Lord, even when it didn't make sense and there was no contingency plan, led to the rescue of an entire nation from oppressive captivity.

If you've been fighting the same battle for years and still can't overcome what enslaves you, I encourage you to stop depending on your own strength. Trust God FULLY. He will never fail you!

CHAPTER 14
THE FAITH OF THE PEOPLE

What are your biggest fears? We all have them, whether we like to admit them or not. I've shared some of my fears while speaking or for the blog I write for, but there are some I've probably kept hidden only because I don't want people to think less of me.

One time, I had a situation where two fears of mine clashed. My wife and I had been blessed with our first home, but it needed some work on the chimneys. The man who came to do the work was someone we randomly picked from the Internet based on reviews. As he was doing the work, I began to fear that he might be taking advantage of us. This was based more on the fact that I knew nothing about chimneys (having never been a homeowner) than the man's quality of work. I called my dad to get some advice and he told me the obvious - that the only way I'd get a better idea of the work the man was doing was to go up on the roof and see it for myself!

While my dad was certainly right, that's just what I was hoping to avoid. You see, I'm even more afraid of heights than I am of getting swindled. I had been on roofs in the past, but the roof at our home is steeper and way taller than any I had ever been on. My dad of course told me this is MY house so it's important for me to know what's going on with it. Again, this was obvious, but not helpful for dealing with my current plight. Ultimately, I chose to get up there and see everything. As I climbed that worker's ladders and walked across the roof taller than any other around us while explaining my fear to the worker, I wondered how pathetic I looked in his eyes!

We like to try to disguise our fears because we worry about what others think. But the reality is that every human being has fears. We know this because fear is connected to sin. In **Genesis 3**, Adam and Eve go from a perfect and fearless relationship with God to being afraid of Him. What causes it? Sin! After they disobey Him and eat from the tree from which God had told them not to eat, the Tree of the Knowledge of Good and Evil, they immediately experience fear, something they didn't even comprehend before. **Verse 10** tells us that after God questions Adam's whereabouts, he admits that he hid from the Lord because he was afraid. The whole thing makes perfect sense. Let me remind you they ate from the "tree of the knowledge of good and evil."

Think about why we fear. I am afraid of heights largely because I'm aware that I could fall and be seriously injured or die. Death and pain only came because of sin. Had I not had that knowledge and had I still been in perfect relationship with God, I'd trust that He would still protect me even from gravity. He'd cause a soft landing, catch me himself, or help me fly! Likewise, I only fear getting swindled by a businessman because I have knowledge that it does happen.

The same was true for the Israelites as they were leaving Egypt and heading for the Promised Land. **Hebrews 11:29** tells us that they "passed through the Red Sea as on dry land" by faith. For the first time in **Hebrews 11**, our hero of the faith is actually a crowd. Just think about what it means for a group of people to have faith. Did they sometimes disagree? Did they have issues? Different opinions? Different perspectives? Different agendas? I'd say so. I mean, most of us can't get through a Thanksgiving or Christmas dinner with relatives without facing some of these things! Yet, there were over two million people in this group.

The people's differences didn't matter. Ultimately, they were united in faith. Guess what? Faith is not about what we "believe." Faith is shown by action. Even if there were some in those two million who thought it was a bad idea to walk through the sea with walls of ocean water on both sides (I'm sure there were), they all chose to walk across. Their faith was not judged by their doubts or differences, but by their ACTION.

The story is in **Exodus 14**. I encourage you to read it, but I want to make a few key points regarding the faith of the people. At first, God speaks directly to Moses and instructs him to tell the people to camp by the sea. This would make them incredibly vulnerable and God even tells Moses that Pharaoh and his army will go after them.

But Moses' responsibility as a servant of God and leader to the people was to pass on God's Word exactly as he heard it, not sugar-coating or changing it to make the people feel more comfortable. Moses had grown in his faith and does just that. He trusts that God will deal with the people's hearts and also that He will protect them as He has been doing the whole time.

At first, the people are completely trusting of Moses and God. But then, **verses 10-12** tell us that the people SAW the Egyptians coming after them and were "terrified." They cried out to the Lord and complained to Moses. In other words, the people were faithful and trusting until they saw and became aware of the great danger. Moses remains steadfast in trusting God, and God tells him and the Israelites to move forward after He has Moses stretch out his staff and part the Red Sea. God could have done it without Moses, but He decided to use Moses because He knew the people trusted more in who they saw (Moses) than who they couldn't see (God).

You could point to any fear you have and see that it comes from the knowledge of good and the opposite of what is good. Even the fear that we all have to some degree, the fear of the unknown, still goes back to what we "know." We fear the unknown because we know that when we don't know something, bad things happen. Did you follow my intentional word play? We relate "knowledge" mainly to what we can see, just as the Israelites did. Therefore, it's not so much the unknown as it is the unseen (they saw the Egyptians, but not the future) that we fear.

Hebrews 11:3 tells us that our faith helps us understand that God created everything that we DO see out of what is NOT visible. But the implication there is that it is not visible TO US. Who is it visible to? Who has never faced an unknown or an unseen? I'm talking about our mighty God! Now, let me ask you, who does a blind person trust? They have to rely on those who can see. So, when we face unknowns or "unseens" in our lives, it makes sense to put our trust in the ONLY One who knows all and sees all. The Israelites knew and saw the sea water and knew the possibility of drowning was there, but God allowed them to see HIS power through Moses so they would trust that the water would stay where it was until Moses again stretched out his staff to return the waters to their place, which ultimately destroyed the Egyptians. This is depicted on the cover of this book.

God knows where you are on your faith journey. If you need to SEE things, God will reveal Himself to you in a way you can't deny. The goal for all of us, however, is to get so close in our relationship with God that we KNOW and sense His presence in our lives and in our difficulties even more than we know the bad things that can happen. When we pay more attention to what we know about God than what we know about the evil in the world, that's when fear turns to faith. I pray that for myself and for each and every one of you each time you face a fear. The One who is unseen is greater than anything we could ever see or understand!

CHAPTER 15
THE FAITH TO BE VICTORIOUS, PART 1

Have you ever been in a situation where you were losing badly and it was going to take a miracle to bounce back and win? If you're a sports fan like me, your mind might automatically move toward a number of miraculous finishes, especially from college and professional football. I can think of half a dozen that I either witnessed myself or heard about from years gone by. The one that most quickly comes to mind is one that happened well before I was born. Because I grew up in a family of fans of the Pittsburgh Steelers, I learned about the play known as the Immaculate Reception at a very young age. The Steelers got a very lucky bounce on the play and came away with an absolutely unthinkable 60-yard touchdown reception in the final half-minute to win a playoff game that would have belonged to the Raiders. NFL Films chose the play as the greatest play of all time. Without that miracle, the Steelers' season was over.

But let's be honest, some of you reading this are in danger of losing a whole lot more than a meaningless football game. As big of a miracle as that was for Pittsburgh Steelers fans like my family members, it meant NOTHING in the long run. They lost the very next week to the Dolphins and their season was just as over as it would have been a week earlier. All this miracle did was delay the inevitable for a week. Some of you need a miracle to keep you from losing your job, your marriage, your children, your mind, or even your faith in God.

The good news is that those who need a miracle are in the same company as the nation of Israel, and truthfully the whole world, which was losing big-time and in desperate need of a miracle 2,000 years ago. They had been promised an anointed Messiah who would come and save them from their misery. The ancient prophets had been speaking about God's truth and His promises for centuries. But then, all of a sudden, the prophecies ended with

Malachi, and a period of 400-500 years that became known as "the silent years" ensued. During that time, there were no known prophets, no direct prophecies about the Messiah, and frankly, not much hope. The Jews were ruled by the Persians at the start of those years and the Romans by the end of them. Those ruling nations were not exactly caring and compassionate. It was a brutal time for the Jews, and they had to wonder if God had ever been real, if he was good, and if he would do what he promised.

As Christians remember and celebrate every year at Christmas time, the miracle that saved the Jews and a dark, hurting world came in the form of a baby born to a virgin named Mary. This truly was an "immaculate conception," and it brought a much bigger victory than an NFL playoff game. Before anyone accuses me of heresy, I understand that the official doctrine of Immaculate Conception has to do with the birth of Mary, not Jesus. But those of us who believe God's Word, which says in **Luke 1:31-37** that Mary would conceive and gift birth to a son by the power of the Holy Spirit overshadowing her, can establish that Jesus' birth was truly miraculous.

We are told in **Matthew 1:21** that Jesus' parents were commanded to name Him as such because he would "save the people from their sins." "Jesus" is the English form of the Greek *Iesous*, which comes from the Hebrew *Yehoshua* or *Yeshua*, which is also where we get the English "Joshua." All of these names, along with several other Old Testament names, can be translated to mean "the Lord saves." Even His very name is there to remind us that He alone holds the keys to victory, but we have to be willing to put our trust in Him even when time is almost running out and we are desperately in need of a miracle to keep us from losing everything. If you have been waiting for God to bring you a miracle to save you but you're losing hope fast, I urge you to stand firm in your waiting and to find comfort in the final words the angel Gabriel spoke to Mary in the traditional Christmas passage I quoted above. **Luke 1:37** tells us that he said, "For no word from God will ever fail." That's an ironclad guarantee, no matter the circumstances.

I'll get into the story more in the next chapter, but a man with basically the same name as Jesus was able to lead the Israelites to a great and miraculous victory over Jericho in the land of Canaan, which was the land promised to the Israelites, by simply believing that God's commands would never fail.

Joshua, son of Nun, had been Moses' longtime servant, but when Moses was prohibited from entering the Promised Land as a consequence for his sin, God called Joshua to be the one to take the Israelites the rest of the way. But it wasn't going to be easy. In fact, the odds would be stacked against them just as they had been ever since God rescued them from Egypt. Then again, it depends on how you view odds. With both Joshua in the Old Testament and Jesus in the New Testament, the WORLDLY odds were stacked against them. Joshua and the Israelites had been wandering in the wilderness looking for a home while they could still be routed by anyone who sought to defeat them. Jesus came as a baby, to a very poor young woman and her husband-to-be, in a dirty manger outside of Bethlehem. But when you add the power of the One who made the universe out of what we can't even see (**Hebrews 11:3**), the odds are greatly shifted. In fact, the enemies have NO SHOT!

Jesus was God in the flesh, but for those who only believed what they could see and had been waiting for a mighty warrior to ride in and conquer their enemies, He was a less-than-ordinary baby who wasn't all that impressive. Only if He truly was "the Lord saves" could He bring a victory to a losing world.

Joshua was a courageous leader, but it's not like he had access to all the chariots and horses he would need to kick butt and take names in Canaan. He and the people of Israel could only be victorious if they trusted in something far beyond themselves, the unfailing word of the Lord who had promised them that victory. When the odds seemed to be against them and they desperately needed a miracle, would they try to take control or surrender fully to the One who could save them?

Hebrews 11:30 tells us that the walls of the city of Jericho fell only AFTER they followed the Lord's seemingly ridiculous command to march around the city for seven days. We'll dig more into the Old Testament description of that event and the things that led up to it in the next chapter. For now, rest in knowing that it is the Lord who saves and brings the victory in all situations. The birth of Jesus is the best reminder and the story of Joshua and the walls of Jericho is a close second. For whatever miraculous victory you desperately need in your life, believe that the Word of God will NEVER fail!

CHAPTER 16
THE FAITH TO BE VICTORIOUS, PART 2

When you lost something important in your life, what were the reasons? When you experienced a victory, what worked? Every now and then, it's good to step back, take inventory, figure out what needs to change, and resolve to do things differently going forward. At the end of the day, however, you will not be able to succeed in making the necessary changes unless you have a plan or steps that you follow.

This is no different than what we see in sports. Often, a TV commentator will give the viewers a certain number of "keys to victory" for each team. The purpose is to identify the steps for each team that would be necessary for them to accomplish their goals. Generally, they are nothing spectacular. They are almost always as obvious as "score more points than the other team" or "stop them on defense and get your offense going."

It's important in any area of life to know what needs to happen in order for us to have success. As we learned in the last section, the most important thing to remember is that we must remain obedient and trusting of the Lord even when we are feeling hopeless and need a miracle to achieve victory. We also learned that "no word from God will ever fail" (**Luke 1:37**). So, in other words, doing what God's Word says is one way to guarantee ourselves success, provided that our goals and definitions of "success" match up with his.

Previously, I briefly introduced you to a man named Joshua from the Old Testament and told you that his name means the same thing that "Jesus" means, which is "the Lord saves." Joshua was leading the people of Israel through the wilderness and toward the Promised Land (then Canaan, but now present-day Israel) after Moses had died. God had a major victory prepared for them that would come through His miracles, but He chose to test their faith first and help them grow and be prepared to win that victory. **Hebrews 11:30** tells us that the faith of the people led to the collapse of the walls around the city of Jericho. Their faith was not just a matter of internal belief. It was shown in their actions as they marched around the enemy's city for seven days, before doing anything else, simply because that was what the Lord commanded. That faith in action didn't come easily, but was learned over time.

We find the story in **Joshua 6**, but the chapters before that help us to see how God was building up their faith every step of the way. **Joshua 2** tells us the story of Rahab. We'll look more specifically at her in the next chapter, but I want to draw your attention to two separate verses that show us the same thing. Rahab lived in the city of Jericho and aligned herself with Israel by hiding the spies when they came to survey the land. We see in **verse 9** that she tells them the reason she protects them is because she knows the Lord gave them the land and all who live there are "melting in fear" because of them. We then see in **verse 24** that the spies go back to Joshua and tell him the same exact thing! God showed them from the very start that they wouldn't have to worry about creating their own victory. They could believe that He was already causing their enemies to melt in fear. So often, we want to control people and make them do or think what we feel is right or best. We must accept that God is always working on hearts, our own included.

Joshua 3-4 then tells us about the moment the people actually entered the Promised Land. The Jordan River, which separated them from the land, was at flood stage. This would be another obstacle for which they had no answer, but God did. He causes the waters to dam up and allows them to pass through the river on dry land just as He had done previously with the Red Sea. It's important for us to note, as **Joshua 4:4-7** tells us, that a member of each tribe of Israel picked up a stone from the middle of the Jordan River to serve as a reminder for them and all future generations of the Lord's great work on their behalf.

Joshua 5 then tells us about a situation that required great trust in the Lord, as well as full obedience and commitment to him. Joshua and the Israelites camped at a place called Gilgal on the eastern border of Jericho. At this point, they are actually IN the Promised

Land. But, just because God promised them something, that didn't mean everyone else would be okay with it. Not everyone is always going to support what God is doing in your life. Sometimes, they'll even fight directly against it. The Israelites expected some of the people occupying the land to put up a fight. They probably kept moving forward wondering why in the world no one was attacking them. But **Joshua 5:1** tells us that it wasn't just the native people who were "melting in fear," but their kings as well!

God gives the Israelites a free path all the way to Jericho, then commands Joshua to circumcise all the males in the Israelite camp right then and there. The reason is that all the men previously circumcised died in the wilderness, so it was time for Joshua to do so with the men who were born during the 40 years in the wilderness. We may not see why this is important, but we must remember this was God's requirement as a sign of faith and trust in the covenant He made with them. Understand that this meant they would have to spend time at the camp waiting to heal from the circumcision. This is in a place where their pagan enemies still lived! They would be completely vulnerable, but Joshua and the Israelites obey the Lord just as He commanded, and He keeps them protected yet again.

After that, we see that they celebrate the Passover, and then begin to enjoy the produce of the land the next day. God had provided manna for the Israelites to eat the entire time they were in the wilderness, but they no longer needed it because they were feeding off the land they had always been promised. Then Joshua has an individual encounter with the Lord. When he is near Jericho, he sees someone who appears to be a soldier ready to attack. Joshua asks if he is for them or their enemies, and the man replies, "Neither, but as commander of the army of the Lord I have now come" (**Joshua 5:14**).

We need to understand this is the Lord speaking directly to Joshua. Who is commander of the Lord's army? That would be THE LORD. Plus, **Revelation 22:8-9** shows us that angels are NOT worthy to receive worship, yet that's exactly what Joshua does once he figures out who he is speaking to. He falls down in reverence, refers to the man as his "Lord," and then obeys the command to take off his sandals because it is holy ground. You'd think God would say that He was on Israel's side, but that wasn't really the issue. It was more important for Joshua and the Israelites to determine if they were going to get on God's side, not the other way around.

The rest, as they say, is history. The Lord told Joshua and the Israelites very specifically what they needed to do to conquer Jericho, and it had nothing to do with fighting at first. They needed to march around the city walls for six days, giving their presence away and again making them vulnerable in the eyes of the world. Then, on the seventh day, they would march around it seven times, give a loud shout, watch the walls collapse, and go into the city and rout those living there. They did everything He commanded and God gave them a great victory. But it all began and grew with the steps of faith and trust along the way.

What can we learn from all this? Joshua and the Israelites had four keys to victory that apply in any battle we are facing in life. First, they died to themselves and trusted the Lord fully when they were circumcised. Second, they celebrated the Passover and remembered the stones from the Jordan River, which were testimonies of the blood of the Lamb and the work God was doing. Third, they ate the produce in the Promised Land, meaning they continued to feed on God's promises and His Word. Finally, Joshua took off his sandals, showing he was fully surrendered to the Lord. The Israelites followed suit when they obeyed the instructions. If any of us keep these four things in our individual lives, we will be victorious in whatever comes our way!

Chapter 17
The Faith of Rahab

Whenever we enter a new season of life, it's a good time to reflect on how we are doing with recognizing our need for the Lord and trusting in Him to get us through anything. You may look back on previous challenges that you faced or you may be anxious as you think about the difficulties that might be coming your way in the future, but faith encourages us to persevere and to learn what trusting fully in God means through each of those things. There's a great old hymn that was redone by Matt Maher called "Lord, I Need You" which reminds us that we don't just need God's presence in our lives on Sunday mornings at church or when we feel overwhelmed by our circumstances; we actually need Him EVERY HOUR!

I remember at the end 2016 when three notable celebrities all lost their lives over a span of four days. After the deaths of George Michael, Carrie Fisher, and Debbie Reynolds, some people that I know publicly mourned their deaths on social media. But what may have begun as typical tributes and remembrances for what those people contributed to the world quickly turned to anger over the deaths. Some people, including several Christians I know, posted things like, "Okay 2016, time for you to go away!" or "2016, you suck!" People would talk about it as if the year itself had something to do with these deaths. Some people couldn't hide their frustrations over these deaths being added to the deaths of people like Prince, Arnold Palmer, and others that took place earlier in the year. I understand that nobody likes death and we all deal with it in different ways, but I was so confused as to how people could throw their anger at a YEAR of all things.

These celebrities were not personally known by the vast majority of the people I'm talking about. Yet, death is something we all have to deal with on a personal level as well. When someone we love is taken from us, how do we respond? Do we throw our anger at God or something else? I believe it's one of the things God uses to get our attention, to remind us of how fragile our lives are and to encourage us to depend on Him. I remember hearing a sermon by John Piper one time when he was teaching on **Luke 13:1-5** and pointed out that when we see great death and destruction, we shouldn't be asking why so many died. He said the more appropriate thing to question is why we have been spared so far! If we truly understand our sin and God's righteousness, we should wonder why we are allowed to live, not why others die.

Faith in who God is gives us a proper perspective. In the Old Testament, a woman named Rahab came to understand who God was even when everyone around her didn't, and it literally saved her life. **Hebrews 11:31** tells us about her faith, which led to her being spared while those who were unbelieving around her were killed. In order to understand the magnitude of her faith in the midst of a disobedient society, we have to go back and read the original story.

In **Joshua 2**, we see that Joshua and the people of Israel are preparing to cross the Jordan River and enter the Promised Land (the land of Canaan that would later become what we know today as Israel). It's only wise to count the cost and see what they might have to deal with when they cross, so Joshua secretly sends spies to scope out the land, "especially Jericho" because that would be the first city they would have to conquer. God was giving them this land, but that didn't mean the pagans who lived there were going to give it up quietly. As we saw in the last chapter, God worked a miracle and caused the walls of Jericho to fall as soon as the people followed His complete instructions. So, this type of reconnaissance didn't really end up being necessary. Nevertheless, Joshua was acting in wisdom and God was going to use it for a different reason.

The reason was to bring Rahab to salvation. She is listed in **Hebrews 11:31** and **Joshua 2:1** as a "prostitute." First and foremost, we must see the truth here that faith is not something that only happens for the "religious" or "self-righteous." It doesn't happen by going to church, and it's not about our parents. No matter where we come from or what we've done, faith is an individual choice and is shown through action. Rahab did a lot of things wrong and lived in a pagan city enslaved by the filth of the world, but she chose to have faith when she came to realize she needed God the most. Her home was a logical place for the spies to go and stay because no one would have suspected anything out of the ordinary. That was their human plan, yet it was foiled and **Joshua 2:2-3** tells us that the men are found out and the king of Jericho asks Rahab to bring them out. They had to be thinking they were toast. They would be killed unless God worked a miracle.

Joshua 2:4-13 then tells us that, at the moment of truth, Rahab lied and told the king that she sent the men away even though they were actually hiding on the roof. The men, who I'm sure were shocked at her choice, then get to hear her reasoning. She shares that she knows the Lord has given them and their people the land, and goes on to say, "The Lord your God is God in heaven above and on earth below" (**v. 11**). This was an amazing statement! A woman with no godly upbringing whatsoever learned what it meant to fear God. When she realized what God was up to, she knew it was time to get on His side. Notice how she said "the Lord YOUR God" (caps mine). Rahab was not yet a follower of God, but she was willing to learn more about what that meant. It started with one step of faith that ultimately saved her and her family. An old pastor of mine used to pray, "Lord, I'm not willing, but I'm willing to be made willing." Sometimes that's all it takes. Yet, we get caught up with religion and judgments. Rahab had no idea what it meant to follow God, but she made her choice and there was no turning back.

Rahab told a lie, and that is never right in God's eyes. But Rahab is not remembered for her sins, but for her faith. In that regard, she's no different than anyone else in **Hebrews 11** or any of us. We all make mistakes and do things wrong, but faith is still a choice each and every moment of our lives. Besides that, we cannot judge people who are not believers to follow a believer's standard. Jesus invites them in. Jesus actually enters the houses of SINNERS. Maybe we should stop judging the actions of unbelievers and start spending more time getting to know them. We never know when that person might make a life-changing decision of faith.

The spies make a deal with Rahab to show them a sign when they come into the city that will tell them she has not changed her mind and is still on their side. Then, **Joshua 6:22-25** tells us that, during the overtaking of Jericho, Rahab and her household are indeed spared because she kept her end of the deal and proved to be faithful. We see at the end of that passage that she "lives among the Israelites to this day." Rahab became a believer AFTER she made the choice to be faithful. She grew in her faith and learned more and more about this God she became aware of. She learned about how much she needed Him in her life every hour. Because of her faith, she becomes so much a part of God's story that **Matthew 1** lists her as one of only four women in the genealogy of our Lord and Savior Jesus Christ.

So again I urge you, stop wasting time judging yourself or others for past mistakes and start trusting God for everything. Accept that you need Him every hour of every day, and let your life be the example that brings sinners to a saving relationship with Him!

CHAPTER 18
THE FAITH OF GIDEON

Have you ever felt like God was giving you way more than you could handle? I'm not sure there is a human being out there who would say "no." We've all been at those points in our lives and many who have at least some knowledge of the Bible immediately think, "Well, either that can't be true or God is a liar because the Word says He will never give us more than we can handle." If you're a Christian and a follower of that Word, and you've come to a point in your life when you just can't take anymore suffering, then you've probably had to go back to that place in the Word to see what isn't adding up.

The verse is **1 Corinthians 10:13**, which really says, "No temptation has overtaken you except what is common to mankind. And God is faithful; he will not let you be tempted beyond what you can bear. But when you are tempted, he will also provide a way out so that you can endure it."

I've been thinking about this a lot recently and I've realized there is a big difference between "handling" something and "bearing" it. As human beings, we want to be in control. We want to have a handle on things. However, when it comes to the battle against temptation, we're not told to handle it or control it by our own willpower. We're told to bear it by the power of Jesus Christ. That's why the last part of that verse says that God will "provide a way out so that you can endure it."

The way out is the Lord Jesus Christ, who demonstrated for us how to bear with temptation (**Matthew 4:1-11** and **Luke 4:1-13**), then defeated death, sin, and temptation by raising from the dead after His crucifixion. Without Jesus, we are still susceptible to those things. But as we walk in the power of our Lord, we can bear our temptations and walk away from them. We do this time after time because we will not be fully separated from darkness and temptation until Christ returns, but the life of a Christian is to be lived to show that Christ is in our hearts even now and with HIS power we can bear with temptation until that glorious day.

One way that we continue to fight this battle and bear with temptation is to remind ourselves of others who have battled and the things that God did to get them through. As we remember the works of God, we gain more confidence and trust that He will continue His work in us. This book on our heroes of faith from **Hebrews 11** has been a good reminder for me, and I hope for you also. The stories of these men and women who were ordinary sinners like you and me help us grow stronger and more committed in our own faith. It's good to pause and consider where we are on this journey.

The writer of Hebrews is now done giving us the details of each person's faith story. He now will give us a few names, knowing that our curiosity is piqued enough at this point that we will do our own research to learn about their faith. In **Hebrews 11:32**, the writer basically tells us he doesn't have time to keep telling us these stories, so hopefully we get the point by now and can study the rest on our own. I wonder why he writes that and frankly, I don't have a clear answer. We don't know for sure who the writer is, but many believe it was Paul. If indeed it was Paul, he seemingly had all the time in the world, having written his other letters mainly while traveling or sitting in prison. Again, maybe he just decided it was time for his audience to do their own study and be blessed!

The first name he mentions is "Gideon." Let me tell you, I was blessed by going back and studying this story, which can be found in **Judges 6-8**. As you can see for yourself if you read those chapters, Gideon enters the scene during a dreadful time for the Israelites, who were God's chosen people. As a nation, they had done evil in the eyes of the Lord, so he allowed them to be overpowered by an enemy, the Midianites. The oppression from the Midianites was so bad that the people of Israel had to go and live in mountains and caves. Then, when they worked hard to produce crops and livestock for themselves, the Midianites simply came and stole everything. After being stuck in their sin for so long, the Israelites finally cried out to God to rescue them (**Judges 6:6**).

God responds first by sending the Israelites a prophet who reminds them of the great things God has done in their history but also reminds them of their sin. It was important for them to see their sin and remember God's faithfulness anyway before they could be released from the hand of the Midianites.

Then, an angel of the Lord comes and appears to Gideon, while he is threshing wheat in a winepress. This was not a normal place to thresh wheat, but it was the only way to try to keep it for himself and his family. **Judges 6:12** tells us that the angel says, "The Lord is with you, mighty warrior." Gideon may have laughed at this. He may have even turned to look behind him to see if the angel was talking to someone else. He sure didn't feel very mighty while he was having to thresh wheat in a private place for fear of the enemy stealing it. After that, he asks an obvious question that we'd all ask: how can the Lord be with us when we're dealing with so much suffering? At that point, we realize it's no longer an angel of the Lord, but the ACTUAL Lord himself who is talking to Gideon. This was an Old Testament appearance of the Christ, who came to assure Gideon that he indeed was with him and was sending him to rescue Israel from the Midianites.

At this point in our reading, we see that Gideon and the Lord then have a prolonged discussion in which Gideon questions the choice (he admits he is basically the weakest in all of Israel), then asks for some signs to show that God really is with them and will deliver the Midianites into their hands. We can learn from this that weak faith is better than no faith at all. Weak faith and insecurity are not heresy. Gideon is still listed among those commended for their faith in **Hebrews 11**, so clearly God can use anyone who puts even a little bit of faith in Him even when we have doubts. God was patient with Gideon and saw the warrior in Gideon that Gideon didn't even see in himself.

Once Gideon discovers it truly is the Lord talking to him, he is given a command that may have seemed like a test to him but was frankly more important than dealing with the oppressive enemy. Gideon is told to destroy the altar to Baal and the Asherah pole that his father and many other Israelites had been worshipping. The Israelites, like many of us, focused more on the external threats and circumstances than their own sin. They continued to worship idols even as they suffered at the hands of Midian. God knew that sin is a far greater oppressor than any foreign enemy, and it had to be dealt with FIRST.

Gideon obeys God and takes down the altars. Once the sin was properly dealt with, he was ready to move forward and accomplish God's will. The enemy would have well over 100,000 troops, yet God planned to use Gideon and only 300 other men to defeat them. God wanted to make sure that stubborn and arrogant Israel did not take credit and boast of their victory, so He had Gideon reduce the army all the way down from 32,000 through two cuts. Once Gideon was down to 300 men, outnumbered over 400 to 1 by the enemy, he was truly ready to let God lead him to victory.

Read the story yourself to see how God does it. Basically, Gideon and his band of merry men were collectively God's tag-team partner. God did all the work, then tagged in Gideon and his army to finish the job and pin the enemy. God caused the enemy to be afraid, which led to them turning on and killing each other.

Gideon had to be tempted throughout the story to walk away from the Lord and give in to fear. But once he understood that the Lord was with him, that gave him power to bear that temptation and endure the struggle. It was power he didn't know he had, and truthfully, he didn't have it until he was obedient and got to know the Lord.

If you are tempted, if you feel like you can't take anymore suffering, if you are overwhelmed by the enemy, then put your trust in the Lord and find the power you need from Him. Faith in Him is the only thing that allows us to endure.

CHAPTER 19
THE FAITH OF BARAK

The beginning of each year brings us to the season of awards shows – the Golden Globes, the Grammys, and the Oscars. While I know they are part of pop culture and appointment viewing for many fans, I've never cared much for them, especially since they have been very politically-driven. But one part of them that I always enjoy is listening to the acceptance speeches. Whether it's one of the awards shows I referenced above or an athletic achievement such as the Heisman Trophy or an MVP award, I love hearing about all the people that worked hard behind the scenes to help the winner get to that place in life.

It's always the person out front with the known name and fame who gets the glory. However, the acceptance speeches give those people the opportunity to give credit where credit is truly due. The ones who work hard behind the scenes generally accept that they don't get the credit because that's the nature of the work they do. But what if they are deserving of the spotlight and still don't get it? Sometimes, a person does the leg work AND produces excellence, but the credit is given to another. How do you react when you KNOW you deserve praise but someone else gets it? Your answer has a lot to do with your level of faith in a God who promises an eternal reward regardless of what we receive on earth.

There was a man in the Bible named Barak who had enough faith in the Lord to proceed and win the victory even after he was told he would not get the credit for it. Because of his faith, he is listed in the group commended for their faith in **Hebrews 11:32**. Like all of the others we have studied so far, Barak did not have a perfect faith. He had at least one moment of weakness that ultimately cost him the honor he would have otherwise received. But God doesn't require us to have perfect faith; He only requires a willing faith that will participate in HIS work to the extent that He commands.

The story can be found in **Judges 4**. As they often did throughout their history, the Israelites were still going back and forth from living by faith to doing evil and worshipping idols. This had a lot to do with their leadership, or the lack thereof. After a period in which they did evil and God allowed them to once again be overtaken by a foreign king and army with 900 iron chariots, the Israelites cried out to God for help.

It's interesting that **verse 3** tells us that Sisera, the commander of the pagan king's army, "cruelly oppressed the Israelites for twenty years" before they finally turned to God for help. How long does it take you to turn to God? How many times do you have to suffer consequences or try all the wrong solutions before turning to the One who you knew had the right solution all along? It's hard to believe they stayed stuck in their ways for twenty years despite their consequences. Then again, maybe some of you reading this have been oppressed by your own sinful choices for even longer.

The great news is that God hears us and responds to our cries no matter how long we have walked away or rejected Him. God brings Deborah, who was both a prophetess and a judge/leader in Israel, to light a fire under someone in Israel who would be willing to put a temporary end to their misery. It turns out that someone would be Barak. In **verses 6-7**, she sends for him and tells him to round up 10,000 men and go up to a mountain top to get ready for her to lead Sisera and all his chariots and troops to the river below where she will give them into Barak's hands. In other words, he has the chance of a lifetime to make a name for himself and win the greatest victory of his generation. How does he respond to this opportunity? Well, he basically says he'll only do it if Deborah goes with him (**v. 8**).

In 2007, I sat in a coffee house in Findlay, Ohio, with an elder from my church in Pennsylvania. I briefly referred to this God-moment earlier in this book. We and a handful of others had traveled to Ohio for the seminary graduation of a friend of ours from the church. I had known for years God was calling me to go to seminary and learn to be a pastor and I knew that would take me to Findlay, Ohio, but this was my first time visiting the seminary and the city. I had been in a little bit of a spiritual rut in my life and wasn't really doing what I was most passionate about despite being a youth leader at the time. The elder and I were talking about life and I was explaining my lack of passion and adventure and he simply said, "Logan, I imagine you will continue to feel that way until you do what you know the Lord is calling you to do." Less than two months later, I began to make plans to move to Ohio and go to seminary. A little over a year later, I made the big move.

As I look back on that moment in my life, what strikes me is that it's not like the elder told me what the Lord was calling me to do. It wasn't his call to make. He only reminded me of what I already knew the Lord was calling me to do. The issue wasn't a matter of confusion about the call for me. It was a lack of faith and a choice I had been making to try to assure comfort if and when I would do what God wanted.

The same is true with Deborah and Barak. In **Judges 4:6**, we read that Deborah tells him, "The Lord, the God of Israel, commands you." The King James version of that verse leads us to believe it is more of a reminder: "Hath not the Lord God of Israel commanded...?" It's a rhetorical question to remind him of something God had already previously revealed to him. Again, the issue was his faith and level of comfort, not the call. When he responded initially, he was only halfway in. Like me, he wanted a comfortable way to follow God's call. But that was soon to change.

Deborah responds to his request by choosing to go with him, but declares that his half-committed response means that he will not receive the honor most would for defeating an oppressive regime, and the Lord would use a woman to complete the job by killing Sisera (**v. 9**). To Barak's credit, he seems to accept this and moves forward in obeying God's command anyway (**v. 10**). The one example we have to show us that Barak grew in his faith throughout this time is that when Deborah tells him Sisera and his army are ready to be overtaken, he doesn't hesitate (**v. 14**). He could stay up on the mountain where it would be tough for Sisera's chariots to reach him, but instead he trusts the Lord and advances down the mountain and wins the victory (**vv. 14-15**). True to the word spoken by Deborah, Sisera is eventually killed by Jael (**vv. 17-21**).

The cool thing is that Barak may not have even had to do too much. **Judges 5:21** shows us that the river where Sisera and his army were actually "swept them away." When we ultimately follow God's commands, even if we initially had very weak faith, God always comes through. He will accomplish things that you and I cannot even imagine on our own. We may not get all or even any of the credit, and someone else who didn't do as much might get it. But we know that the victory is ultimately God's anyway so it's irrelevant which human being is honored.

When we move forward in faith, we get to watch and participate in what God is doing in the world. If you know God wants you to do something different or take a big step of faith, now is the time. Don't expect Him to show up and show off until you've taken that step out of your comfort zone.

Samson / *Judges 16:28-30*
"'Sovereign Lord, remember me. Please, God,
strengthen me just once more, and let me with
one blow get revenge on the Philistines
for my two eyes.' Then Samson reached toward
the two central pillars on which the temple stood.
Bracing himself against them, his right hand on the one
and his left hand on the other, Samson said,
'Let me die with the Philistines!'
Then he pushed with all his might,
and down came the temple on the rulers
and all the people in it.
Thus he killed many more
when he died than while he lived."

Chapter 20
The Faith of Samson

I used to be a pastor at a small rural church in Ohio for about three years. During the course of my time there, we never had a true worship leader or music team as some churches are accustomed to having. However, that didn't stop us from worshipping the Lord. When I first got there, a friend of mine who had experience with drums but did not see himself as a singer was actually the one to get up on stage each week and lead the congregation in singing worship songs off the computer. Eventually, my wife, who has an amazing voice, was willing to take over the singing duties each week. When she wasn't there, however, myself and my friend who had led in the past occasionally led worship together. It was the first, and ONLY, church where I was able to sing on the worship team. God made me a lot of things, but a singer isn't one of them. Yet, I learned a valuable lesson from that experience, and my friend who viewed me as his pastor and mentor actually set the example for me. We joked that neither one of us could carry a tune in a bucket, but together we sounded much better than individually. It was a good lesson in teamwork, but the bigger lesson for me was that God uses even our weaknesses.

Most of us know our own strengths. We are aware of our weaknesses but rarely talk or even think about them. We're so focused on what WE are able to do that we rarely stop to think about what GOD is able to do when our ability just isn't there. As we continue to look at the heroes of the faith in **Hebrews 11** in order, we come to a man who was quite possibly one of the strongest men who ever lived. But, despite that overwhelming strength, he was commended for his faith in God that he showed when he was weakest in the physical sense. In **Hebrews 11:32-34**, one of the names mentioned is Samson, and the description of what was accomplished by faith that most clearly fits his life is "weakness was turned to strength." As with all the other heroes, we must look back to learn and find hope for the future.

The full story of Samson can be found in **Judges 13-16** and I encourage you to read the whole thing. I'll touch on certain parts of it so we can understand his weakness and his faith. Because Israel was still going back and forth from following God to doing evil in His eyes, God allowed them to be overtaken by one of the most notable enemies of the Israelites in the Old Testament - the dreaded Philistines. We see that before Samson was even born, an angel appeared to his mom and explained that she would have a child who would "take the lead" in delivering his people from the hand of the Philistines (**Judges 13:5**). What's interesting is that it doesn't say he will be THE deliverer. He will start the process, but there's almost this understanding from the very beginning that he will not complete it. This shows both God's omniscience (He knew the sins Samson would commit and their ultimate consequences) and His omnipotence (despite Samson's failures, God was able to use others to complete the deliverance). The circumstances of Samson's birth, how he would be raised, and his parents' knowledge of God suggest that Samson had a great spiritual foundation on which to build his faith.

If we can learn anything from Samson's life, it might be that a great spiritual foundation alone does not make one faithful. Each person is responsible for his or her own choices. Even when we seemingly have all the advantages, we should remember, like the old Progressive commercial says, to "be careful, because that kind of power can go to your head." Samson's actions as an adult reveal that he may have thought he was invincible. He marries a Philistine woman in **Judges 14** and even when his parents try to remind him that it's unacceptable, he simply says, "She's the right one for me."

While God was certainly using this situation for his ultimate purpose of confronting the enemy of Israel (**v. 4**), that doesn't excuse Samson's giving into temptation. But let me stop and address that for a minute. Why would God need to confront the Philistines Himself? Apparently, there was no one in all of Israel who was willing to do it. Samson was supposed to lead that charge and instead married one of their women. It seems like he kind of went the other way on that one!

It's no wonder that Samson was basically comfortable in his sin and figured he could walk outside of God's commands and still receive God's blessings. The entire nation and culture was doing it! With Israel's previous enemies who ruled over them, there was ruthless oppression and forced labor, but we don't read of that with the Philistines. It's like everyone was accepting of the status quo, which was the people of God living together with the unbelievers, but the unbelieving culture was ruling over everyone and the people of God were comfortable with it. Does this remind you of any particular culture or nation? God is always looking for a leader who is willing to lovingly confront and challenge a culture that desperately wants to drag people away from Him and enslave them. We cannot let ourselves remain comfortable with our sin!

In the chapters that follow in the book of Judges, you can see how Samson's comfort with his sin leads him down a path of destruction. He breaks every part of the Nazirite vow that his mother had taken for him before he was born, gets drunk, gambles, deals with a nagging wife who ultimately sides with her own people the Philistines against him, calls her a heifer, kills a bunch of people in order to pay his gambling debt, and feels justified and invincible through it all. His own people hand him over to the Philistines, but he is able to break loose and kill a thousand Philistines with the jawbone of a donkey. This only strokes his ego and feeling of invincibility even more, so he forgets that his mighty strength comes from the Lord. He ends up in a sinful relationship with a pagan woman named Delilah. He is infatuated with her, so she plans to use that against him. She seduces him to the point where she is able to tie him up and let the Philistines take him captive. He seems to enjoy the seductive games she is playing, probably because he feels nothing and no one can defeat him. But **Judges 16:20-21** tells us that his sins eventually catch up to him as the strength that God had given him is taken away and he ends up being captured by the Philistines, who gouge out his eyes, bind him in shackles, and take him to their prison.

This seems like the lowest of lows for the man God called to deliver His people from the Philistines. Not only did he not do that, he now finds himself without eyes and totally at the mercy of the enemy he was born to defeat. They force the imprisoned Samson to perform for them at their parties. He is a laughing stock and a total failure in the eyes of many. But it is precisely in that moment of his blindness, submission, and total weakness that he remembers that God had given him all the gifts he had in the first place. He remembers that while his circumstances had changed, God was still God. As he is placed between the pillars at the Philistine temple, where thousands of people are gathered, he cries out to God and asks for the strength to be returned to him just one last time so he can kill many Philistines in his final breath. God grants him this dying wish and gives him enough strength in that moment to bring down the entire temple and kill thousands of people who worshipped pagan gods (**Judges 16:23-30**).

Samson could have just focused on all his failures and basically quit life. But in his biggest moment of weakness and despair, he chose to focus on what GOD could do rather than what HE could not do. If you have fallen into sin and the consequences have weakened you, or if you simply sense that you don't have what it takes to accomplish a task God has given you, know that GOD alone has all the strength you need. If you put your faith in His ability over your own, you will accomplish great things even in weakness!

CHAPTER 21
THE FAITH OF JEPHTHAH

In the winter of 2018, the Super Bowl and the Winter Olympics, two of the most popular sporting events, happened within the same week. What makes these two events so great is not merely the games themselves but all the mental, physical, and even spiritual preparation leading up to them and the stories of triumph and perseverance that are told in the lives of the participating athletes. In the Super Bowl in 2018, we had the New England Patriots and the Philadelphia Eagles. Though I hate to admit it because I can never root for them, the Patriots are better than any other team in the NFL at taking players who have been rejected, used up, or overlooked by other teams and making them into key contributors and stars. The Eagles were a significant underdog in this game but continued to win despite their damaging injuries. They moved forward with a backup quarterback that no one else wanted. Likewise, the Olympics are full of participants from all over the world who have continued to get back up after injuries, rejection, and failures. Even if you hate sports, these events teach us important life values.

One of the things that is required to go from the bottom to the top in the world of athletic achievements is FAITH. If you're competing in an individual sport, you have to have faith that your hard work and ferocious training will eventually yield results. You have to accept delayed gratification. A team sport requires not only that same faith in your training and practice but also faith in your teammates to do their jobs while you do yours. Because each of these areas of faith are not foolproof, meaning they occasionally fail an athlete, we often hear stories and professions of faith in the only One who does not let us down - the Lord Almighty. For those professional and amateur athletes who trust in Jesus more than their own abilities, even the darkest moments of rejection and failure in their sport cannot defeat them for good.

As we continue in this book on our heroes of the faith, we come to a man who was despised and rejected through no fault of his own, but put his trust in the Lord to win a great victory. In **Hebrews 11:32**, we are told of someone named "Jephthah." His name may be one of the hardest to say, but there is no doubt that the honor bestowed upon him by the writer of Hebrews was well-deserved. Like the others before him, Jephthah was commended for his faith despite his imperfections. **Hebrews 11:33** tells us that the aforementioned group of faithful ones "through faith conquered kingdoms, administered justice, and gained what was promised." All three of those faithful accomplishments certainly fit the life of Jephthah.

Judges 11 tells us the story of Jephthah. We learn some important things about Jephthah right off the bat in **verses 1-3**. We see that he was considered a "mighty warrior," but that he was the illegitimate son of his father, Gilead, because he was born of a prostitute. Clearly, Jephthah had nothing to do with this and was the product of his parents' sinful choice to commit adultery. Yet, as was often the case in those days in Israel, his status was held against him. His half-brothers (the legitimate sons of Gilead and his wife) drove Jephthah away and said he would not get any of the family's inheritance because of his birth to the prostitute. In other words, they rejected him completely and had no use for him. But we know God loves to use those who are of no use whatsoever to others. While human beings often only want us when they need us, our God has a plan for us from before we are even in our mothers' wombs (**Psalm 139:13-16**).

Jephthah came along during a time when the Israelites had once again worshipped idols and made God angry enough to allow them to fall into enemy hands. They were ruled and oppressed by the Ammonites and the Philistines. Just as we saw in the last chapter that God used Samson to confront the Philistines, he was about to use Jephthah to take out the Ammonites.

It's interesting how the Israelites' relationship with God mirrored the relationship between the people of the town of Gilead and Jephthah. In **Judges 10:10-14**, we see that the Israelites as a whole cried out to God to rescue them, and after constantly rescuing them before, He tells them this time that they are on their own and should cry out to the false gods they've been worshiping to save them. But, after they humbly submit to Him and choose ACTUAL REPENTANCE by getting rid of the false gods in **verses 15-16**, God has compassion on them again.

Once God's plan to rescue the Israelites is in full swing, the people of Gilead are looking for someone to lead them into battle in **Judges 11**. The wise choice is the "mighty warrior," Jephthah, so they go to him. Like God, he first reminds them of how they rejected him. Like God, he recognizes that they only want a relationship with him when they desperately need him. Like they did with God, the people humble themselves and offer to make him head over all of Gilead.

Now, it's important for us to see the difference between God and man. God waited for true repentance from the Israelites but needed nothing else after that and longed to rescue them because of His compassion. When it came to Jephthah, the people needed to sweeten the deal to get him to come to their aid. Jephthah then makes them basically take an oath that they will truly let him be their leader at a place called Mizpah (**v. 11**), which not coincidentally is the same place that Jacob and Laban made a binding agreement in **Genesis 31:49**. The name of the place meant "watchtower," and it was thought that one did not go back on his word there because the Lord would see it.

The next part of **Judges 11** records Jephthah's conversation with the king of the Ammonites and shows that his faith was in the Lord to bring the victory. He explains to the enemy king that any land that the Israelites possess was given to them by the Lord God of Israel. In **verses 23-28**, Jephthah recognizes that this battle is a spiritual one first and foremost. He encourages the king of the Ammonites to take whatever land their pagan god gives them, and Israel will take whatever land their God gives them. He declares that they will let the Lord, the Judge (with a very intentional capital "J"), decide their dispute over the land. Since the king of the Ammonites does not listen, Jephthah then leads an army and overtakes them. God gives this despised and rejected man from birth a great victory, proving that no one is "illegitimate" in HIS eyes.

Jephthah shows his weakness and imperfections with first making, then stubbornly keeping, a foolish vow to the Lord in the rest of the chapter. We can all form our opinions about those verses and many scholars have. For now, I'd rather leave you with what is not an opinion, but God-breathed Scripture. "Isn't it obvious that God deliberately chose men and women that the culture overlooks and exploits and abuses, chose these 'nobodies' to expose the hollow pretensions of the 'somebodies'?" (**1 Corinthians 1:27-28** [The Message])

We know for a fact that God used Jephthah, a faithful man who was considered "illegitimate" by his own family, to defeat one of Israel's oppressive enemies. No matter how others in your life have treated you, is there anything that God can't also do in your life? Leave the opinions of others in the past and start trusting, following, and obeying the Lord today!

David and Goliath / *1 Samuel 17:45*
"You come to me with a sword, with a spear,
and with a javelin. But I come to you in the
name of the Lord of hosts, the God of the
armies of Israel, whom you have defied."

CHAPTER 22
THE FAITH OF DAVID

In a perfect world, human beings would just automatically do exactly what God says because He said it and there is nothing to distract us or make us think we should not obey. That's how God created things when Adam and Eve were first made, and ultimately the world will be returned to that utopian place when God unveils the new heaven and the new earth for those who knew and loved Him. For now, we continue to live in our sinful world with our own fears and selfish hearts.

The amazing thing is that God still uses us to accomplish His great works, even as we doubt Him or turn away from Him. Sometimes, we just need a little bit of extra motivation to do what we already know He has told us to do. When I was in college, I remember being in a Bible study where four of the five guys in the group had either started or continued going to church because of a girl that was there. Our Lord certainly knows how to reel us in!

Each of those men from that group are now married to women they met through church or Christian functions and they are serving the Lord in amazing ways. One of them lives in South Korea with his wife as missionaries, two are teachers (including that missionary), two are pastors, and one manages a ministry at another college. Several of us still get together to encourage one another every year though we graduated 15 years ago! To think that God used our desires to have girlfriends to either bring us to church or keep us there long before we even knew each other makes me laugh and smile. God will do his work one way or another, and He's not opposed to use whatever He knows motivates us!

One of the greatest heroes of the faith was also initially moved to action by extra motivation beyond just doing what God wanted. I'm talking about David, a man about whom we learn a lot throughout the Old Testament. To try to put the faith and life of David into a short chapter is a difficult task, but we can learn a lot about him from possibly the most frequently referenced Bible story of all time, both inside and outside the church.

Hebrews 11:32 counts David among those who are commended for their faith, but we really begin to see that faith play out all the way back in **1 Samuel 17**. The Israelites and Philistines are preparing to battle each other, but it likely wasn't going to happen as long as everyone on the Israelite side continued to cower in fear at the sight of Goliath, a monster of a man who defied God and the Israelites and even mocked them daily. But God was waiting and urging someone to step up by faith and defend His name and His people. This was the occasion for David to make a name for himself by honoring God's name and putting his full faith in Him.

We do have to understand something about this story. We have to realize that Goliath was a messenger of Satan who literally took his physical stand against God twice a day every day (**v. 16**). Look at Goliath's measurements and his armor in **verses 4-7**. He was six cubits tall, had six pieces of armor and weaponry, and the iron point of the spear was six hundred shekels in weight. You can either believe it's a coincidence, or you can look at those numbers, 666, as if the Word is telling us about Goliath's role in Satan's great plan. If Goliath could kill David, Satan could eliminate the bloodline from which the Messiah would eventually come, take away Israel's occupation of the land where the Messiah would eventually be born, and ultimately try to defeat the Messiah. Satan already knows it's a lost cause, but it doesn't stop him from continuing to rebel and try any way that he can to thwart God's plans and promises. Anyone who would defeat this giant messenger of evil would surely be doing God's work.

At the time of this story, David was just a young shepherd boy and the people of Israel had chosen Saul as their king based on his outward appearance. Saul was their king because he was their biggest and baddest dude. Yet, when they desperately needed someone to stand up to Goliath, "Saul and all the Israelites were dismayed and terrified" (**v. 11**). People generally follow their leader. If a leader shows cowardice, he can't expect the people to find courage. Saul had been lacking leadership for a long time ever since he started walking away from the Lord and loving his own self and his position too much. Because the Lord was no longer with him, he had no faith or bravery to go after Goliath and the Philistines. A new leader was needed.

That new leader literally arrives on the scene in **verses 12-26**. Because David was the youngest and forced to tend the sheep at his father's home, he wasn't able to fight in the Israelite army and was just going back and forth between the two people he was serving, Saul and his father Jesse. His father orders him to take food to his brothers who are on the battle line with the Israelites. When he does this, Goliath comes out and shouts his usual mockery while David is still there. This is the first time David hears it and it's almost like he is shocked no one has done anything about it yet. In **verse 26**, he says, "What will be done for the man who kills this Philistine and removes this disgrace from Israel? Who is this uncircumcised Philistine that he should defy the armies of the living God?" David cared not that Goliath was so tall. He wasn't bigger and better than God. The rest of the Israelites were terrified and saw themselves as little grasshoppers compared to Goliath, but David saw Goliath as a mere grasshopper to God!

Notice how David, who was full of faith in God, still had a slight ulterior motive. He figured he could serve and honor God and get a great reward in the process. Like I said before, God is not opposed to using other motivation to get us moving. David was told that Saul would give anyone who kills Goliath great wealth, his daughter in marriage, and tax exemption. I find it more interesting to note what Saul was NOT willing to give up - his throne. Here was Saul, a man bigger and stronger than all of Israel, yet still a wimp who was afraid to stand up to Goliath while desperately trying to hold onto his throne against ALL threats, including BOTH Goliath and David. Then there was David, a man who had no reason to even get involved in this mess until he heard someone talk about his God in a demeaning way and also heard what he could get out of the deal. One was a leader by name and title; the other was a leader by faith.

David goes on to defeat Goliath with a simple sling and a stone - the greatest upset in all of history. But it wasn't, especially when you consider who was on David's side. The people looked at David vs. Goliath and said there is no chance David can win. David looked at

Goliath vs. God, using David as a mere servant to accomplish his purposes, and said there is no way God can lose. David went on to receive all that was promised him and all that motivated him, plus the throne of Saul. He never boasted about his conquests except to give glory to God for the victory.

What are you facing right now in your life? Where are you afraid to move forward because there is an evil giant staring you down? Learn from David and choose to see the God that is on your side. When you do, you'll see that it's not you, but that enemy giant, who has absolutely no chance!

CHAPTER 23
THE FAITH OF SAMUEL

I remember when the TV show American Idol, which became one of the most popular television shows of all time, first came out and one of the biggest reasons to watch the show was Simon Cowell. He was quite the polarizing figure because while other judges were soft, kind, and tried not to ruin the contestants' dreams, Simon seemed to have no problem telling them exactly what they needed to hear. His goal was not to placate the contestants just so they could leave that week or the entire show feeling better about themselves. His years of working in the industry taught him that the best thing he could do for those people was tell them the truth.

Whether you liked Simon or not probably had a lot to do with how well you receive the truth when it is not what you hoped it would be. Personally, I enjoyed watching Simon on the show because I felt that he was the only person that truly cared about what was best for the individual. As I relate it to my own life, I've had plenty of "yes" people around me who were unwilling to give me the dose of reality I sorely needed at times, and I've also had plenty of people who were always willing to tell me the truth even when they knew it would sting temporarily. I can say with 100% certainty as I sit here and type this that the truth-talkers have been much more beneficial than anyone who wanted to make me feel better in the moment.

I'm sure many of you would say the same thing if you sit back and reflect on your lives. The truth doesn't always feel good, but it's never wrong. We can look at accepting truth when it doesn't feel good as a sort of discipline. **Hebrews 12:11** tells us, "No discipline seems pleasant at the time, but painful. Later on, however, it produces a harvest of righteousness and peace for those who have been trained by it." Hearing what we need to hear gives us a chance to get back on track. If what we hear has to do with sin, it also gives us the chance to repent.

In this chapter, our faithful hero is a man from the Old Testament named Samuel, which literally means "heard by God." I'll get into the circumstances of his birth later, but it helps to know that his very existence was brought about by a conversation between his mother and the Lord, and that his life from very early on was characterized by his own ability to speak to and hear from God Himself.

Samuel is the last hero mentioned by name in **Hebrews 11**, but his story is quite unique. It's hard to place him within one specific era in Israel's history because he was around at the end of the period of the judges and the beginning of the period of the kings. Samuel is most known as one who "called upon the name of the Lord" (**Psalm 99:6**). As such, Peter also lists him first among all the prophets as he is addressing the crowd in **Acts 3:24**. Like all of the other heroes of the faith listed in **Hebrews 11**, Samuel had a role to play in God's story. But unlike many others, he had no great military victory or conquest. His role was to simply speak truth where it was needed, and he did it well.

The first time we really see Samuel doing what he was called to do is in **1 Samuel 3**. He was only a boy but had been set apart for the Lord's service by his mother. Basically, that means he was living at the house of the Lord and serving under a priest. That priest's name was Eli, and the story tells us that Eli had wicked sons and that he did not properly deal with their sins. If the priest was not even willing to address sin within his own family, then he certainly wasn't honoring the Lord and the position he had been given.

Samuel hears God speak to him for the first time, but it's bad news. God tells Samuel, who I remind you is STILL A BOY, that he is going to judge Eli and his household for the sins of his sons which Eli knew about and did nothing. **1 Samuel 3:15-18** then tell us that Samuel was afraid to tell Eli about the vision the next morning despite Eli's insistence. This is where we see, however, that Samuel does not allow that fear to stop him from honoring God's word to him. He tells Eli the truth, the whole truth, and nothing but the truth, and Eli correctly accepts the word of the Lord knowing he can't change it anyway. **Verse 20** then tells us that all of Israel recognized Samuel as a prophet of the Lord.

We see more examples of Samuel's willingness to speak the truth throughout **1 Samuel**. In **chapter 8**, we see that the elders of Israel ask for a king to lead them so they can be like the other nations. This greatly disturbs Samuel, so he goes to the Lord. He's probably expecting God to work something good in the situation, but God just tells him to give the people what they want and warn them of the dangers of naming a king to rule over them, which really meant they were no longer looking to God for guidance but a mere man. Samuel again pours his heart out sharing everything God told him to share, but the people reject his words and demand a king. Repentance is rejected by the people, so they get Saul as king and the downward spiral begins.

In **chapter 12**, God brings thunder and rain when Samuel is done speaking to the people about God's greatness and their sins. The people repent and admit their sin of asking for a king and also ask Samuel to pray that they won't die for their sins. This might be where Samuel says something like, "Heck no! You knuckleheads have rejected my preaching so many times that I am done with you!" But that's not what he says. He tells them it would be a sin against the Lord for him to fail to continue praying for them. Samuel continued to be faithful to God's word.

Samuel stands up to King Saul several times, including in **chapter 15** when Saul fails to completely obey the Lord, who told him to completely destroy the Amalekites. Saul destroys everything and everyone that is weak and despised, but he keeps the best of the best alive. He tries to pretend his intention was to sacrifice them to the Lord, but Samuel declares that God prefers obedience over sacrifice every single time. He is so serious about keeping God's word that he even kills the king of the Amalekites himself when Saul is unwilling.

In **chapter 16**, Samuel anoints David as the next king of Israel even when he is rejected by everyone else, including his own father and family members. Samuel honors the word of the Lord for the rest of his life, and actually, beyond! In **1 Samuel 28**, Saul is so distressed (sin will catch up to you eventually) that he consults a witch to contact the spirit of Samuel long after he has died. A crazy thing happens and the witch, probably to her own amazement, is able to bring up Samuel. Saul asks Samuel for help and guidance and even the spirit of Samuel continues to speak the difficult truth of God's word to Saul.

What we can learn from Samuel is that God's word is never to be sugar-coated. Without understanding the reality of what God is saying to us, we can never repent, and repentance is a MUST for anyone to really turn to Jesus. God sets a very high standard for those who claim the responsibility of speaking HIS word. Throughout the Bible, He condemns those who speak only what the people desire to hear so they can feel great about themselves.

Samuel kept his faith in God's word and never manipulated it to be what he wanted. He continued to speak it and very seldom brought about repentance. But as a true prophet, his ONLY responsibility was to speak the truth. The results were up to God. This is a powerful lesson for any of us who share God's word with others. In case you didn't know it, faithful Christian, that's not just preachers; IT'S YOU TOO!

CHAPTER 24
THE FAITH OF THE ANONYMOUS

Every human being likes to be recognized for the good things they have done and would prefer to remain anonymous regarding any mistakes that have been made. It's part of our sinfulness and selfishness that exists deep within us. When we begin to follow Jesus, the hope is that the opposite begins to occur. When we see that Jesus was followed by a crowd with a very false perception of Him and that He was hated anytime He even hinted at His true identity, we must accept that being His disciple doesn't guarantee us fame, fortune, or recognition. It doesn't guarantee us that life will be trouble-free. In fact, in the story of Christianity, the worst possible thing happened to the best possible man!

As followers of Jesus, we ought to be willing to ignore any chance at getting credit and always direct it toward our Lord and Savior. When we make mistakes, that's when we ought to be willing to identify ourselves. The Apostle John tells us that confessing our sins allows us to be forgiven and purified (**1 John 1:9**). In the next verse, he tells us that claiming to be without sin makes Christ out to be a liar (**verse 10**). So, when we try to prevent exposure of our sins just to keep a good name for ourselves, yet still seek recognition for any good deeds, we're actually harming the reputation and name of Jesus.

My very first real job when I was 16 years old was what's called a "costume character." At Hershey's Chocolate World in Hershey, PA, I was paid to dress up in a variety of candy bar costumes and walk around and greet people. We did whatever we could to put a smile on people's faces, including dancing, posing for pictures, dribbling a basketball in costume, or messing with people's hair. Regardless, it was all done anonymously. I am in thousands of pictures all over the world, but no one knows it's me. I was even in a commercial as the Hershey Bar, and no one knows it's me. I could dance like a fool or accidentally wreck one of the displays that were set up, and no one would know it was me. I didn't get credit for anything good, but I didn't get blamed for anything terrible. It was all that dumb Kit Kat Bar! Looking back and knowing the entirety of my work there, it's probably a good thing I was anonymous!

The same is true regarding my faith journey. Sure, my selfish ego would love to be recognized for any good things that God allowed me to accomplish. But if that would also mean that all my sins and failures are publicly known, I'll pass. Since our sins and missteps far outweigh our good deeds, I'll go ahead and assume that most believers out there would feel the same way I do.

As we read **Hebrews 11** and then look back at some of the stories of the heroes of our faith who are mentioned by name, we are reminded of both their successes and their failures. Those individuals were not looking to be made famous. They were merely walking their own personal journeys of faith. I wonder how they'd feel today about their stories being told in full. Would David want everyone to know that he defeated Goliath with a sling and a stone even if it meant they'd also know that long after that, he committed sins with Bathsheba and against her husband that had horrific consequences for all involved? Samson is on a whole different level. If I were him, I wouldn't want my story told at all! Those are just two examples, but I try to put myself in the shoes of each person and I wonder how they'd respond to the notoriety.

We've reached an interesting point in this book, as we have now gone through all of the individuals who have been mentioned by name. But the stories of faith in **Hebrews 11** don't end there. After Samuel is the last one mentioned by name, we are told of the accomplishments of many others through faith. The stories were most likely known by many in the writer's intended audience. Whether or not the writer of Hebrews mentions their names, those people and their stories were known to the Jewish people. So, why keep them anonymous?

We are not 100% sure of who wrote the book of Hebrews, but the fact that so many faith stories are mentioned without a person's name attached to them is one reason why I believe the writer was the Apostle Paul. When you think about other things Paul either wrote or said, he's pretty intentional about telling anyone who will listen that it's always about Jesus and never about us. It's recorded in **Acts 20:24** that Paul said, "However, I consider my life worth nothing to me; my ONLY aim is to finish the race and complete the task the Lord Jesus has given me - the task of testifying to the good news of God's grace" (caps mine). In his letter to the Philippians, he writes that "to live is Christ and to die is gain" (**Philippians 1:21**), and later talks about all his reasons to boast, yet says he considers them "garbage" or "dung" compared to knowing Christ and even participating in his sufferings (**3:7-11**). Those are just a few examples, but Paul was always exemplifying that our achievements, our sins, our lives, and even our very names are irrelevant and only the goodness of God's grace through Jesus needs to be made known.

In the coming chapters, I will be addressing these "anonymous" accomplishments by faith. I will put some names to them because that's really the only way we can go back and learn more about the context and story behind the faith. But I wanted us to have this chance to pause and consider what is most important.

If you have a chance to walk by faith and accomplish something great, do you find yourself looking for the credit? Do you trust God with your reputation, or do you try to control what others think of you? Like many of the heroes of faith found in the Old Testament, you may go through something difficult only to bring glory to God. It might not have anything to do with YOU and your reputation. Truly trusting in God means being faithful even in the aftermath. It means focusing on Christ's story over our own. God may call you to a life of faithful anonymity. Could you accept that? If not, take a look at your own sins and ask yourself whether you'd really want everything exposed. I know I wouldn't, and that makes it undeniable that Christ's story is a much better one to tell than my own.

CHAPTER 25
THE FAITH OF HEZEKIAH

What bothers you enough to make you want to fight? In this day and age, it seems a person can't talk about politics or religion without making someone else so aggravated that they could actually threaten or cause bodily harm to the one whose view offends them. When I was growing up, people didn't seem to get all bent out of shape about those things like they do now. That probably has a lot to do with the more recent explosion of social media and 24-hour access to the Internet and news updates than anything else. We had to find real things to get upset about when I was growing up. The line generally got crossed when someone talked about someone else's "momma." When a person couldn't get under your skin by insulting you alone, he had to turn his attention to your mom and sometimes even your dad.

We were taught growing up that words were never enough to start a fight. That old saying, "Sticks and stones may break my bones but words will never hurt me," was basically branded in our minds. Of course, everyone knows it's not entirely true. Words do hurt and they are often the catalyst for violent conflicts. Still, we were taught to walk away from someone who was picking on us, ignore insults, and refuse to come back with violence.

As we begin to look at heroes of our faith who are not mentioned by name in **Hebrews 11**, the first one who comes to my mind is a man who had to stare down hurtful words of not his mother and father, but worse! His entire nation and their God were being put down by the Assyrian king, Sennacherib. **Hebrews 11:33-38** tells us all of the things that the anonymously faithful were able to accomplish, overcome, or endure through their faith in the living God and His promises. The first thing mentioned is that they "conquered kingdoms." This could be describing a number of different people, some of whom we've already acknowledged in this book. In this chapter I want to tell you about King Hezekiah.

The story begins in **2 Kings 18:17** when Sennacherib sends several of his delegates to King Hezekiah in Jerusalem to threaten them. His delegates speak what they're told by their king, which is nothing but an attempt to intimidate Hezekiah into surrendering to Sennacherib and the Assyrians. Hezekiah evidently had some level of confidence because he had honored the Lord (**verse 19**), but the Assyrians were intent on destroying that boldness and instilling fear. Hezekiah knew that fear is a liar and his faith allowed him to stand firm in the midst of this threat and fear-mongering that was happening.

Sennacherib's message to Hezekiah in **2 Kings 18:19-35** is basically that he shouldn't have any confidence in the Lord or anyone else because no god of any other nation that has been conquered has been able to stop Sennacherib and the Assyrian advances. The thing that Sennacherib ignored that Hezekiah remembered is that our God isn't like any other god. We know that Hezekiah remembered this because **verse 36** tells us that his delegates "remained silent and said nothing in reply because the king had commanded, 'Do not answer him.'"

Isn't that sometimes the hardest thing in the world to do? When someone is threatening us, putting us down, or mocking those we love, all we can think about is what we can say or do to shut them up. But that isn't always what God wants. Let me say it differently: it's almost NEVER what God wants. He tells us through James, the brother of Jesus, "My dear brothers and sisters, take note of this: Everyone should be quick to listen, slow to speak, and slow to become angry, because human anger does not produce the righteousness that God desires" (**James 1:19-20**). In other words, we should always be slow to respond even when someone is really irritating us or saying hurtful things.

Hezekiah could have felt like it was all up to him to defend the name of God. He could have put himself on that pedestal. But instead, by faith, he remembered who God was and who he wasn't. He let Sennacherib and his minions threaten, mock, and ridicule them. He even let them mock the Lord their God. Why didn't he respond? It's simple, really. Hezekiah had the necessary humility to be a human king who submits to God, and he understood that God didn't need anyone to defend Him. Hezekiah knew that God could look out for Himself, and any fool who would mock Him was only signing his own death warrant.

Hezekiah not only acted in faith personally, but he led by faith when he commanded his delegates to not even respond to Sennacherib's obviously idiotic statements. In **2 Kings 19**, Hezekiah goes to the prophet Isaiah and asks him to seek the Lord on behalf of the nation. He admits that they are in distress over the threats facing them but still leaves it in the Lord's hands rather than walking by fear. Isaiah seeks the Lord and promises Hezekiah that the Lord will take care of Sennacherib and have him killed without Hezekiah or his army even having to lift a finger (**verse 7**). Sennacherib sends messengers to Hezekiah one last time with one final threat and mocking of our great God in **verses 9-13**. After that, Hezekiah goes to the Lord and basically tells him, "Take care of your light work, God." He reminds God of the ridicule sent from Sennacherib (**verse 16**), declares that Sennacherib was only able to destroy other nations and their gods because they were "only wood and stone, fashioned by human hands" (**verse 18**), and then implores the one, true living God to deliver them from Sennacherib's hand so that the whole world will know who really is the living God (**verse 19**).

When we put the ball on the tee for the Lord, he knocks it out of the park every single time. Hezekiah could have focused on his own strengths and won a great battle to improve his own popularity. If he had made it about himself, he would have surely been destroyed. He accepted that his situation was hopeless without God, but with God victory would be a certainty unless God wanted them to be defeated temporarily, in which case nothing they could do would prevent it anyway. When his native people and living God were mocked and threatened, Hezekiah resisted the temptation to respond and sought the Lord. May we all take such an approach to those who want to harm us, be it physically, verbally, and even on social media!

CHAPTER 26
THE FAITH OF JOSIAH

How hard would you be willing to work with no guaranteed tangible reward whatsoever? Most people know what their jobs pay them and know exactly what they get for any extra work that they do. If they do the work, they expect to be paid fairly. The Bible even tells us this is a good and right concept. Jesus Himself said, "Stay there, eating and drinking whatever they give you, for the worker deserves his wages" (**Luke 10:7**). This was what He told His disciples as He was sending them out to minister. Many Christians know the quote "the worker deserves his wages," but they don't remember the first part. Sometimes, we're called to do work and to accept WHATEVER the reward is. It might be a million dollars, it might be nothing, or it might be something in between. Either way, the work almost always gets done before the reward is given.

This is especially true when talking about work that is right in God's eyes, or even work that He has commanded us to do. The thing we all have to decide for ourselves is whether we are willing to do whatever is right in His eyes, no matter the cost, with the knowledge that He commanded it being the ONLY reason to do it. That's where the rubber of faith meets the road of life. Today, we look at an unnamed hero of the faith who was willing to do what God said JUST BECAUSE He said it.

In the last chapter, I wrote about King Hezekiah and his refusal to cower in fear to the threats and ridicule of Israel and the living God, as well as his leadership during that time. Hezekiah's faith may have had an impact on those who knew him or heard the stories of what God did through his leadership. But two people who clearly didn't care about his faith enough to follow in his footsteps and faith were his son and grandson. The two kings who immediately succeeded Hezekiah were his son Manasseh, and then after that, Manasseh's son, Amon.

2 Kings 21 tells us briefly about their reigns as king, but the most important thing to know about them is that they did evil in the eyes of the Lord and worshiped idols. Hezekiah had destroyed all the idols that previous kings and generations had worshiped, but Manasseh decided it was a good idea to go through all the effort to rebuild them. Hard work and effort can be completely wasted if they're toward ends that are not pleasing to God. Manasseh reigned for 55 years, so his detestable practices led his people into sin for a long time (**v. 11**). After he died, Amon simply followed in his dad's evil and his reign only lasted two years before he was assassinated by his own officials (**v. 23**). Because the kingship was passed through the blood line, it had to go to Amon's son, despite the fact that he was only 8 years old! His name was Josiah, and he's our next hero of the faith.

Whether it was because Josiah wasn't old enough to understand or enjoy the fleeting pleasures of sin that his father and grandfather pursued or because someone spoke truth into his life to turn him toward God, Josiah chose to go back to the glory days of his great-grandfather Hezekiah's reign and worship the Lord only. **2 Kings 22:2** tells us, "He did what was right in the eyes of the Lord and followed completely the ways of his father David, not turning aside to the right or to the left."

I find two things about this verse fascinating. First, it lists his father as "David" even though we know his biological father was Amon. That shows us that David was his "father" in the sense that the faith tradition which had been ignored by the previous generations began all the way back at David's reign. Secondly, it says he didn't turn aside to the right or to the left. I'm sure this has nothing to do with the author's purpose for that statement, but isn't it interesting that "right" and "left" are the two words used to characterize the intense division in our politically-crazed and agenda-driven nation? This one verse in the Bible ought to remind us that NEITHER side is always right in the eyes of the Lord!

I consider Josiah one of the unnamed faithful heroes in **Hebrews 11** because **verse 33** says that the faithful "administered justice." Now, that's what the NIV translation says. However, I realized that another translation I look at from time to time, the NKJV, says they "worked righteousness." This is where any knowledge we can gain from the original Greek is critical. In our language, those two phrases are not as synonymous as they are in the much broader Greek language where words can mean a number of different things in English. So, I did some research in my dusty old *Greek New Testament* from seminary. While "administered justice" would not be wrong, it appears the more accurate representation here is "worked righteousness." This would especially be true if applied to Josiah and the work that he did.

I encourage you to read **2 Kings 22-23** to see all that King Josiah did during his reign. I'll try to give you a brief overview. In the 18th year of his 31-year reign, he sends his secretary to the high priest at the temple of the Lord so that those working hard to repair it are fairly and honestly compensated. While his secretary is there, the high priest tells him that he has found the Book of the Law in the temple. This suggests that previous generations didn't care to read it or follow it, and we already know that is true. The secretary takes it back to Josiah and reads it in his presence.

This is the life-changing moment for Josiah. As he hears the Law of God, he can't bear the thought of how long his throne and the people of Judah have been far from God. He recognizes that the Lord has every reason to be angry with them and seeks the Lord through a prophet about how they should respond. The prophet tells him that disaster will be brought on the nation and its people because of their disobedience, and all Josiah is promised is that he will actually die BEFORE any of the disaster happens so he doesn't witness it. If I'm Josiah, I'm thinking, "Gee, thanks, Lord!"

Josiah then decides to read the Book of the Law in front of the entire nation of people and calls for them to renew their covenant with God. The people do so, but then Josiah gets to work. **2 Kings 23:4-24** then tells us how Josiah systematically destroyed all of the idols of the pagan gods his people had been worshiping and even killed some of the priests who made sacrifices to those gods. One of the idols he destroyed was for the god Molech, to whom human child sacrifices were made (**v. 10**). Not only does Josiah destroy everything that was evil in the eyes of the Lord, but he also restarts the observance of the Passover to the Lord (**v. 21**), which had been commanded in **Exodus 12:24-27**, yet had not been observed for many generations. You see, true repentance and fear of the Lord has to do with not only eliminating the sins of commission, but also the sins of omission. If you haven't done what God says, it's time to start.

Make no mistake about it, the work that Josiah had to do was long and hard just to get his people back on track. I'm sure it didn't make him happy to slaughter the unrepentant priests. I'm sure he had people ridicule or hate him for tearing down their precious statues. But he knew this was what was righteous in God's eyes and he was committed to "working righteousness" back into the nation for which he was responsible, no matter how hard it would be.

We would think that after everything he did, he'd be blessed and things would end well for him. But it wasn't so. **2 Kings 23:26** tells us that God did not change his mind about bringing disaster on the nation of Judah, and then **verse 29** tells us that Josiah was killed by the king of Egypt in battle. So, God kept his promise to Josiah and spared him from having to witness the destruction of his people and country. But still, it doesn't seem to us like a fair end to Josiah's story. He reigned 31 years, meaning he died at the age of 39. It wasn't like he slowly went to sleep and never woke up either. He was killed in BATTLE, so it was no fun at all. He received no tangible reward for his faith.

Back to one of the original questions: Is doing the right thing in the eyes of the Lord enough for you? Do you need something more? It's a question of faith and total surrender to Him that only you can answer.

Chapter 27
The Faith of Caleb

Have you ever planned to do something that you were absolutely certain God had set in your heart to do? It could be a dream or passion that you believe He gave you, a command you feel you have to follow that came directly from God, or a promise He guaranteed for you if you simply trusted in Him every step of the way. Anyone who has walked with the Lord for any period of time can probably point to a season of their lives where they were following a plan they thought God had created just for them only to find that nothing but obstacles stood in their way. How we respond to those obstacles is a matter of faith versus fear.

A story out of college football and the annual NFL Scouting Combine from a few years ago further illustrated this. A young man from the University of Central Florida by the name of Shaquem Griffin, who dreamt of playing in the NFL, was able to bench press 225 pounds 20 times and also ran the fastest 40-yard dash time in the history of the combine for linebackers. He also had a wonderful college playing career that culminated with him being named Defensive MVP of the Peach Bowl in 2018. While these accolades would be impressive for any athlete dreaming of making it to the NFL, they are exaggerated by the fact that Griffin had his left hand amputated when he was just 4 years old! Observers at the bench press said they'd be surprised if he was able to do even 5 reps, but he blew them away by getting 20 even with a prosthetic hand to grip the bar. Shaquem Griffin has had a dream of playing in the NFL since he was a kid, destined to join his twin brother who is already there. But even if he felt it was his destiny, his resolve was tested with the obstacle of having one less hand than everyone else. His passion, desire, and hard work has allowed him to face that obstacle and many others with faith rather than fear. That year, he was drafted by the Seattle Seahawks, who already employed his brother.

I have no idea if Shaquem Griffin is a follower of Jesus Christ or not, but I do know that his determination in the face of adversity is an example to all of us, especially believers. When God gives us a command or a promise, it's not even about chasing our own dreams and desires at that point. We have something even greater.

In the Old Testament, God had promised Abraham and his many descendants in Israel that they would be given a land of their own, a land flowing with milk and honey. This would become known as the "Promised Land." To experience God's promises, we are generally required to take some action. God often works in a way that includes us. When Moses was leading the Israelites through the wilderness and they knew they'd be approaching the Promised Land, he was told by the Lord to send men from each tribe of Israel to explore the land of Canaan, which was the Promised Land. Moses obeyed God and ordered the men to go just as he had been told to do (**Numbers 13:1-20**).

When the men who went to spy on the land returned, the difference between walking by faith and by fear was all of a sudden crystal clear. **Numbers 13:27-29** tells us that most of the men first talked about how the land indeed flows with milk and honey just as God said it would, but then immediately turned their attention toward the obstacles, which included fortified cities, lots of enemies, and some very large people who would be impossible to defeat in their eyes. It was at this moment that one of the spies, a man named Caleb who represented the tribe of Judah, decided he had heard just about enough of this malarkey. According to **verse 30**, Caleb "silenced the group," stood up before Moses and everyone else and said, "We should go up and take possession of the land, for we can certainly do it." This took some serious guts, but more importantly, serious faith. Caleb was probably a little stunned that his countrymen could be so easily driven away from God's promise by a few obstacles. Unfortunately, Caleb's attempt to steer them back onto the road of faith fell on deaf ears, and the men continued to live in fear and even "spread among the Israelites a bad report about the land they had explored" (**v. 32**).

We should not miss what happened there. The spies who allowed their fear and negative circumstances to cripple them weren't just content with keeping it to themselves. They made sure everyone else knew how they felt. In general, even when we're wrong, we try to win the popularity contest. Even when we're wrong and caught up in sin, we need to get as many people on our side as we can. It changes nothing about truth and reality, but sure does make us "feel better." This has been a problem with humanity for thousands of years. Today, just like back then, the only way out of this problem is to re-focus our eyes and hearts on God's truth and promises.

Caleb, this time with help from Joshua (the same one who would later take over as leader of Israel after Moses died), tried again to dissuade everyone else from their fear and negativity. In **Numbers 14:6-9**, Joshua and Caleb tore their clothes in front of the entire nation of Israel and then proceeded to remind everyone that the land they explored was "exceedingly good" and that it had everything God promised it would have. The tearing of their clothes was a common expression of intense grief. How sad they must have been to see that they were in the minority led by faith while their friends and family members crumbled in fear! After reminding them of what they saw in the land, they spoke about the need to stay on God's side in order to receive His promises. They pleaded with the people to not rebel against the Lord.

Sadly, even this plea did not change the hardened hearts of the Israelites. True to the words of Caleb and Joshua, the rest of the men who spread the bad report about the land never actually got to receive the promise of God. They were struck down by a plague and died in the wilderness (**Numbers 14:37**). However, because of Caleb's faithfulness and Joshua's support of it, they alone from the group who explored the land were kept alive by God until they could physically enter the Promised Land themselves.

Caleb is not mentioned by name in **Hebrews 11**, but the writer tells us in **verse 33** that some of the unnamed faithful heroes "gained what was promised." There is no question that this description would fit Caleb among others in the Old Testament. The good news is that it can fit you too! In a world where people, even many in the Church, are held back by fear and circumstances that appear impossible, you can stand up and gain what is promised by reminding others of God's faithfulness, his power, and his promises if we simply walk with Him, obey Him, and trust Him completely. No matter how big the giant is, your God is bigger!

Daniel in the Lion's Den / *Daniel 6:22*
"My God sent his angel, and he shut the mouths of the lions.
They have not hurt me, because I was found
innocent in his sight. Nor have I ever done
any wrong before you, Your Majesty."

CHAPTER 28
THE FAITH OF DANIEL

"The world is a very poor critic of my Christianity, but it is a very sufficient one of my conduct." -Alexander Maclaren

In my Men's Devotional Bible from Zondervan, there is a piece written about "habits of holiness." It tells of a cigarette manufacturer years ago that invited people to take a 30-day test with their product. They relied on the idea that anyone who used their cigarettes for 30 days would develop a new habit and most likely become addicted to their specific brand. The writer goes on to remind us that the same is true with good habits such as flossing, exercising, eating healthy foods, doing devotions, watching our language, etc.

This got me thinking of the annual season of Lent. Some Christians have habits that display a lack of discipline for the rest of the year, then focus on making positive changes during Lent. I'm not rejecting the notion that we ought to take advantage of every opportunity to motivate ourselves to make positive changes in our lives, but I do think that sometimes we put too much emphasis on our own human will. We think we can just put our minds to something and we'll be able to accomplish it.

When it comes to the habits God wants us to have in our lives, we can't just flip the switch in the moment of crisis. This chapter's hero of the faith who is not mentioned by name in **Hebrews 11** is Daniel, a man who certainly didn't wait until the crisis came to practice good habits in his relationship with God.

In **Hebrews 11:33**, we see that some of the ancient faithful ones "shut the mouths of lions." There were several other men to whom this phrase could apply, but writing about Daniel was an obvious choice for me. Here was a young man who had most likely witnessed the killing of his family members and many friends along with the destruction of his city when the Babylonians came and overtook Jerusalem. As if all that wasn't enough, he very likely was made a eunuch once he was taken as a captive to Babylon because that was the case for most court officials and those who served the king. This is a level of devastation that most of us can't even imagine and don't want to. Yet, even in a foreign land as a captive, he continued to view his relationship with the Almighty God as one that would sustain him.

After many trials and some dream interpretation, Daniel is made one of the top three advisers to King Darius (**Daniel 6:2**). At this point, he is the definition of an overcomer, having already defied the odds to reach a level of prominence no one thought possible. But that kind of worldly success breeds jealousy from those around you. The officials, who were probably getting tired of hearing how amazing Daniel was from the king, decided they needed to find some way to accuse him. They tried and tried only to find that there were no skeletons in Daniel's closet. I mean, stop and think about that. How long would it take someone to find a scandal or some other conduct or character issue if we told them to dig into the background of any politician? Probably about two minutes!

When these people couldn't find a legitimate reason to accuse Daniel, they decided to go ahead and create one. In **Daniel 6:4-9**, they convince King Darius to put a new decree into writing that stated that anyone who worshiped any god or human being except the king over a period of 30 days would be thrown into the lions' den. In other words, they appealed to the king's ego and it worked. These people did this knowing that Daniel prayed multiple times every day and likely wouldn't stop.

They were right. **Daniel 6:10** tells us that Daniel changed nothing even after he heard about the decree. He was at peace and it was settled in his mind that God was truly in control no matter what happened. That verse also tells us that Daniel opened his windows toward Jerusalem and prayed three times a day. He clearly wasn't trying to hide it. He also got down on his knees, showing humility, and gave thanks to God, showing gratitude. The jealous ones immediately report him to King Darius and remind him that once a decree is in writing, it cannot be altered (**vv. 12-15**).

We read that Darius tried everything he could to save Daniel, but ultimately was not willing to go against the law and against his own foolish word. When he ordered Daniel to be thrown into the den in **verse 16**, a very interesting thing happened. He said, "May your God, whom you serve continually, rescue you." This is the heart of the quote I placed at the beginning of this chapter. People may not understand our "religion" or our God, but they certainly know how to recognize good and bad behavior in us. The jealous officials and the pagan King Darius all knew they could find no wrongdoing in Daniel's life. Darius even acknowledged that Daniel "serves God continually." When those who are against our faith or don't have our best interests in mind are still able to commend our conduct and recognize our commitment to God, we're doing something right.

But Daniel was committed long before any of the crises came. He daily spent time in prayer before the Lord and kept his focus on God and His plan. As captive as Daniel was, he lived in more freedom than anyone else in this story. **Daniel 6:18** tells us that Darius couldn't eat, drink, or sleep for the whole night knowing Daniel was in the lions' den. He knew he had made a dumb decision and he also knew Daniel was a good man that he didn't want to lose.

So, what's the rest of the story? Daniel had a better night's sleep than Darius! The lions didn't touch him and Daniel gave credit to God for sending an angel to "shut the mouths of the lions" (**Daniel 6:22**). Daniel had started new habits in his life and kept them to the point where he couldn't even imagine a life where he didn't pray to God at least three times each day.

When we start things God wants us to start, we can't imagine how it will all be done. But once it has become a habit, we don't even consider not doing it. Daniel's heroic faith was on display for all to see. **Verse 19** tells us that Darius rushed to the lions' den as soon as he woke up to call out to Daniel to see if he was safe. That tells me that Darius, who didn't even know God, practically expected Daniel to still be alive. He knew what God was capable of and actually believed there was a solid chance that God might save Daniel from Darius' own hand. If he believed there was no way Daniel would survive it, then why would he rush to the den with anticipation?

Do you want to have the kind of faith that is THAT noticeable to those around you? Do you want to be so faithful that even those who have no faith practically expect God to work in, through, and for you? If so, begin your habits of spiritual discipline now. Stick with it until it becomes something you can't live without. Read the Word, spend time in prayer, even fast when applicable. Remember that God is in control, and living a life that trusts Him completely for results is the most peaceful and stress-free life you'll ever find!

CHAPTER 29
THE FAITH OF DANIEL'S FRIENDS

One year on Resurrection Sunday, I started wondering about which day is the most important one in the Christian faith. My immediate thought was that it is obviously Resurrection Sunday. But then I started thinking about it and an argument could be made for any of a number of days. Some of you may feel Christmas is the most important since Jesus could not have been our perfect sacrifice if He hadn't been born of a woman and lived as a human being. Others may feel Good Friday is the most important since our penalty was paid that day. I suppose Pentecost could be the answer because even Jesus Himself told the believers to basically do nothing but wait in the city until they received the power of the Holy Spirit (**Luke 24:49**). Maybe this is a ridiculous question and the most important day hasn't even come yet because it's the day Christ returns. Truthfully, they are all important days and it's a matter of personal preference or experience which one you place at the top of the list.

For me, I will still go with Resurrection Sunday as the most important. I think of it as the ultimate realization that nothing in this world truly has power over us. On Good Friday, Jesus paid the wages of sin that we deserved (**Romans 6:23**), but He demonstrated power over it by rising from the grave on the third day. It wasn't just power over sin; He also demonstrated power over death, pain, and suffering. Our Savior and Lord endured one of the most cruel, ruthless, and inhumane punishments until He decided it was time to give up His very breath, then showed us on the third day that even the most cruel, ruthless, and inhumane circumstances don't have any power over Him whatsoever. As we become His disciples and receive His Holy Spirit, we also can live knowing we have ultimate power over even the worst types of suffering.

I remember when I was a child there were a few occasions when my mom would ask us what we thought would be the worst ways to die. It was more of a curiosity thing than a need to pursue morbid discussions. What I remember is that myself and my family members generally agreed that being burned alive and drowning were right at the top of the list. I don't know if they are worse than the crucifixion, but I do know that God addresses both of them when he promises to save the Israelites: "When you pass through the waters, I will be with you; and when you pass through the rivers, they will not sweep over you. When you walk through the fire, you will not be burned; the flames will not set you ablaze" (**Isaiah 43:2**). While not every Israelite would experience this verse literally, there was a group of people for whom it seemed like the words were a direct and specific promise.

In **Hebrews 11:34**, we see that some of the faithful heroes who are not mentioned there by name "quenched the fury of the flames" by faith. There isn't a lot of mystery regarding which heroes from the Old Testament would fit this description. They were the friends of Daniel and their names were Hananiah, Mishael, and Azariah. Unless you know your Bible trivia, your first thought is, "Who?" These were Israelites who, like Daniel, probably watched all of their family members get killed and most of their property and towns destroyed during the Babylonian invasion. As they were taken captive and forced to go back to Babylon along with Daniel and others to be in the king's service, they were renamed Shadrach, Meshach, and Abednego (**Daniel 1:6-7**). There's a good chance you've heard those names, but maybe you never even realized that the names by which you identify them are actually the names given to them by a pagan official!

I'd love to be able to tell you that having their names changed from something Godly to something pagan was the worst thing that happened to them, but that just wouldn't even be close to the truth. Many of us learned the VeggieTales story of "Rack, Shack, and Benny" in the fiery furnace when we were children, but knowing only that story without the background could cause us to miss the essence of their faith.

You see, they were in the "fire" long before they stepped into the furnace. Their faith wasn't about making the courageous and right decision in their one big moment. As it was for Daniel, the faith of these three young men was about making God-honoring choices each and every day. In addition to having name changes forced on them, they dealt with the loss of loved ones, forced captivity, forced service to the king which very well may have required them to be made eunuchs, and having to learn a new pagan culture just to name a few things. When Babylon conquered Jerusalem, these guys instantly faced more pain and suffering than most of us do in a lifetime.

The biggest thing we see about their faith throughout all of this is something we DON'T see. They did not complain or try to fight any of it even one bit! They had to go through three years of pagan training before they could even serve their pagan king, yet it's as if they accepted it all as part of God's plan. I'm sure they had their moments of grief since they were human beings, but we see in them a faith that not only intellectually believes God is ALWAYS in control but lives as such with confidence. It's because they knew God was in control no matter what their circumstances showed that they were unwavering in their story of heroic faith.

After King Nebuchadnezzar built a 90-foot golden statue to represent HIS kingdom and demanded that all bow down to worship the statue (**Daniel 3:1-6**), Shadrach, Meshach, and Abednego kept in mind GOD'S kingdom and knew He was in control over Nebuchadnezzar. They trusted that God would do whatever was necessary to bring Himself glory in this situation and they were not concerned with their own lives.

They refused to worship the idol because it was against the commands of their God, plain and simple. They didn't try to lead a revolt. They weren't even disrespectful to the king who had taken so much from them. They simply chose to obey God rather than man. As a matter of fact, they didn't even feel a need to defend themselves. **Daniel 3:16-18** shows that they had total peace knowing that either God would rescue them so the flames didn't harm them, or He wouldn't and their temporary pain would end with death anyway. They trusted that God alone knew what was best. They could stand firm in obeying Him and let Him worry about the results.

Nebuchadnezzar threw them into the furnace, but true to the prophecy from Isaiah, they didn't get burned. Three young men were bound and thrown into a blazing furnace, but seconds later, four men were seen walking in the furnace "unbound and unharmed" (**Daniel 3:21-25**). The fourth is believed to be either an angel or Christ himself. When Nebuchadnezzar had the men leave the furnace, there was evidence of God's total protection and control. **Daniel 3:27** tells us, "They saw that the fire had not harmed their bodies, nor was a hair of their heads singed; their robes were not scorched, and there was no smell of fire on them." Complete faith in God allowed them to "quench the fury of the flames." God was in control all along and all they had to do was actually walk in that knowledge.

I encourage you to reflect on this truth as it relates to the resurrection. Just as God was in complete control when Daniel and his friends were taken captive, He was in control in the fiery furnace. Just as God was still in control on Calvary, He was in control when Jesus rose from the grave. Just as God has been in control in these absolutely horrible circumstances, He's still in control in your life. Walk in it and let Him worry about the results!

CHAPTER 30
THE FAITH OF ELIJAH

Ehrich Weisz was just a young boy when his family moved to America in 1878. According to his Wikipedia page, he got his first job as a performer when he was just 9 years old and would go on to accomplish things that no one else in his field ever had. He started out as a trapeze artist, but at the age of 17 became a professional magician. He worked his way up through the ranks and eventually, needing something to make a name for himself, began experimenting with escape acts. For the purpose of becoming more widely-known, Ehrich changed his name to Harry Houdini. He started with escaping from handcuffs and shackles and even challenged local police to lock him in jail.

As others began to imitate him, he had to keep getting more and more daring to attract the crowds. His escape acts moved on to straitjackets, then being locked in an over-sized milk can filled with water, then inside nailed packing crates in water. If he failed, he died. Later, his most notable acts included escaping from the ground after being buried alive six feet deep. The first buried alive stunt almost cost him his life. Houdini was so committed to his show that even when he had a ruptured appendix and a high fever while in Detroit in 1926, he did not cancel an event or seek medical attention. Unfortunately, this led to his death just a short time later at the age of 52. After all his great escape acts, he had met his match. Even the great Harry Houdini could not escape death!

In **Hebrews 11:34**, we're told that some of the faithful anonymous were able, by faith, to "escape the edge of the sword." These would include David, Samson, and others about whom I've already written in this book. One man who has not yet been covered in this series and who certainly fits the description in that verse is the prophet Elijah. He didn't just escape the edge of the sword one time; he made a habit out of it.

1 Kings 16:29-34 tells us about the moral landscape, or lack thereof, in Israel when Elijah entered the scene, compelled by the Lord who had prepared him for such a time. King Ahab had taken over in Israel and "did more evil in the eyes of the Lord than any of those before him" (**v. 30**). The passage goes on to tell us that he considered the sins of previous kings to be "trivial." He built altars and temples to pagan gods such as Baal and Asherah, and he married Jezebel, who was the daughter of a pagan king from another nation. Immoral leadership begets immorality and a total disregard for the things of the Lord. So, it's no surprise that we read in **verse 34** that Hiel of Bethel rebuilt the city of Jericho at the cost of his oldest and youngest sons, in accordance with Joshua's oath after God had allowed the Israelites to siege Jericho in **Joshua 6:26**. It's in the midst of this incredible decline of morality that God sends Elijah to Israel.

The first thing Elijah does is go directly to King Ahab and tell him that it won't rain in Israel for the next few years except at his word (**1 Kings 17:1**). This would cause drought and famine like you've never seen before. Ahab and Jezebel wouldn't be very happy about this and, because they had completely lost touch with the reality of God's authority over them and the nation, would blame Elijah for the bad circumstances. In the rest of **1 Kings 17**, as a matter of protection and faith-testing for Elijah, God commands him to leave where he is and go to a ravine in the woods, where he will drink from a brook and be literally fed by ravens who bring him his daily supply of food. Elijah, likely knowing that Ahab and Jezebel will find a way to kill him, puts his faith in the Lord and decides he has a better chance of surviving with God in the wilderness than with whatever comforts and protections he had trusted before.

Eventually, God takes away the brook and the ravens and commands Elijah to go to a widow in Sidon, the same region where Jezebel had actually come from, to get his food and water. Elijah had already ignored his tradition which said that he couldn't eat something that came in contact with an unclean animal such as a raven, and now he'd have to ignore the tradition that said he couldn't go into the home of a Gentile woman. Elijah was faithful and God used him to heal the woman's very ill son. In the process, Elijah got his daily needs met and saw that he could trust God.

This was especially important when God then told him in **1 Kings 18** to go and present himself to Ahab. How would you feel if God told you to go say "hi" to the person desperately trying to kill you? But Elijah didn't hesitate and did what God said (**v. 2**). However, Elijah and Ahab did not come face-to-face until God used Obadiah to bring them together. Obadiah was a man who, despite being an administrator to Ahab, had courageously hid a hundred of the Lord's prophets while Jezebel was doing everything in her power to kill as many of them as possible (**v. 4**). When Elijah meets him and tells him to notify Ahab that he is there, Elijah even has time to reconsider, to doubt, or to have second thoughts. Yet, he remains faithful to God and to Obadiah, waits until Obadiah tells Ahab, and then presents himself to Ahab.

The meeting leads to the great confrontation between Elijah and the prophets of Baal at Mount Carmel. Ahab gathers all of the 850 prophets to join Elijah. It's one against 850, yet Elijah has God on his side. Elijah urges the people to stop wavering between two opinions and to follow ONE God. Since the people give no response at all, revealing that they are complacent in their sin like many today, Elijah encourages the face-off. After the prophets of Baal try to call down fire on their sacrifice and there is nothing but crickets, Elijah calls for God to accept his sacrifice and God does. Elijah then makes certain that the prophets of Baal are all slaughtered for their sin against God.

What Elijah does to the prophets of Baal enrages Jezebel all the more, and she swears by her gods that she will kill Elijah within the next 24 hours. Elijah knows that Jezebel and Ahab now have more reason to kill him than ever before, so he begins to fear and runs away (**1 Kings 19:3**). God continues to provide for his basic needs even after he runs, but then God shows up and literally asks him what he is doing (**19:9**). Elijah explains his reason to the Lord, mainly that all of the other prophets of the Lord has been killed and now they are trying to kill him too. God shows his power to Elijah through natural disasters and a gentle voice, then asks Elijah the same question again. Elijah answers Him the same way and God tells him to go anoint the next kings (**19:15-16**). Finally, God promises that He has reserved seven thousand people for Himself in Israel who have not turned to Baal. Elijah trusts Him and his faith is back on track.

Neither Jezebel nor Ahab ever did get another chance to kill Elijah as far as we know. Jezebel vowed to make it happen, but no matter where Elijah was, he was always safe in the arms of the Lord. Elijah didn't need to defend himself against those who meant harm toward him. God was his defender and provided for his needs everywhere he went, even when he ran away before God wanted him to. Some of us may trust God when it comes to small things, but Elijah learned to trust God with his LIFE. As long as he was doing what God commanded, he had no reason to believe that God would let him die one second before God was done with him.

Do you struggle with a fear of death? Are you a parent that is overprotective of your children because you're afraid of what might happen to them, even when they go to school? Once you accept that God is way better at protecting you and your loved ones than you are, you'll be ready to put your full faith in Him. Elijah's faith allowed him to escape the sword even when he had every reason to fear it and avoid it. God will lead you to the same freedom.

CHAPTER 31
THE FAITH OF ESTHER

In the movie *Open Range* from 2003, Kevin Costner's character gives us one of those "mic drop" quotes before he walks away from a bar conversation. In the discussion, a group of men are talking about the great injustice that is happening in their town. Costner's character, Charley Waite, mentions that they could do something about it and a father stands up and says he doesn't want his sons getting involved because they could be shot and killed. Charley then stands up and says, "You may not know this, but there are things that gnaw on a man worse than dying." He walks away leaving this group of men to think about whether the present issue is one that matters enough to them to be willing to die for it.

We all have things and people we think we'd be willing to die for, but we wouldn't really know for sure until the moment presented itself. As you think about your life now, is there an injustice in the world for which you'd be willing to give it up? Is there a cause that matters enough to you? Does the will of God matter enough to you? We know that the will of God to make the necessary sacrifice on our behalf to cover our sins mattered enough to Jesus to go through with it even though He knew the suffering and was even tempted to give it up (**Matthew 26:39**). But there were many people even before Jesus who were willing to give up their lives for God's will if necessary.

The book of Esther tells us the story of one such person. The title character rose to prominence from humble beginnings during a very difficult time for not only herself but also the entire nation of Israel. She would fit the description of faithful heroes in **Hebrews 11:34** "whose weakness was turned to strength." Her "weakness" was not something she was born with. Rather, the difficult circumstances that God allowed in her life led her to a point that would break absolutely anyone. **Esther 2:5-7** tells us about it.

As you may recall from the chapters about Daniel and his friends, all of the Israelites were either killed or captured when King Nebuchadnezzar and his Babylonian army invaded and overtook Jerusalem. The events of Esther take place well after that, as King Xerxes of the Persians is now the authority, but the Jews are still in captivity. We learn that Esther was originally named Hadassah, but like Daniel and his friends she was given a pagan name in the pagan place. She has been raised by her cousin, Mordecai, who had been carried off in exile, because both of her parents had died. The verses don't tell us for certain, but it's very likely that her parents were among those murdered by the Babylonians. On top of all that, Esther is a stunningly beautiful young woman, which wouldn't have necessarily been a blessing given that she is around evil, immoral men with no one really to protect her.

King Xerxes was a very foolish man who literally banished his previous queen from his presence just because she refused to parade herself immodestly in front of him and his drunk friends (**Esther 1**). Several years later, he and his attendants came up with this plan to find a new queen. Basically, they would round up the most beautiful virgins from all over the Persian empire and have them each come to the king and spend one night with him after they've had many months of beauty treatments. Just in case it isn't already apparent to you, those poor girls didn't spend that night watching movies and eating chocolate, and they didn't have the option to say "no" to anything that happened. Their purpose was only to please the king as best they could. This is what we call "rape." They could dress it up and make it seem like a privilege for the girl and do whatever else they want to make it seem normal in their culture, but do not ignore the evil that existed and the fact that it was commonplace in this immoral kingdom.

I also want to point out that it's not like the king suddenly decided to start forcing women to sleep with him. He already had a harem of women that he could call on whenever he wanted. Like everyone, however, the king started getting bored with his sin and had to take it to the next level. After everything else that has happened in Esther's life, now she is taken from the one family member who she had left and forced to live in the king's harem until it was her turn to go and try to please him. Yet, her life is an example to all of us that even the evil deeds of human beings can be used by God to bring about His will. He doesn't cause it or approve of it, but He does show His dominion over sin by accomplishing His purposes anyway.

As the story goes on, Esther is picked out of what scholars believe was about 400 women and is chosen to be the next queen. **Esther 2:17** reminds us that it wasn't even about love, but that the king was "attracted" to her more than any other woman. Later in **Esther 3**, we read about the plot of a man named Haman, who had been elevated to the king's second in command. He wants everyone to kneel down and pay him honor in accordance with the king's order, but Mordecai boldly refuses since doing so would be a sin against God. He seems to be following in the footsteps of Shadrach, Meshach, and Abednego.

Mordecai doesn't lead a riot. In fact, he had exposed a plot to assassinate the king earlier. He is willing to submit even when he disagrees or doesn't like the king's decisions, but the stopping point is when obedience to the king requires disobedience to God. Haman decides he is not just going to kill Mordecai, but ALL of the Jews (**Esther 3:6-15**). The king gives the edict and the plans are set in place.

Up to this point, Esther has not revealed her true nationality to the king or to anyone else. She has been waiting for the right time and Mordecai sends word to her in **Esther 4:8** that basically, it's now or never. It was time for her to reveal her ethnicity and her people to the king and beg him for mercy. Initially, she responds out of fear and says that if she approaches the king without being summoned, he can have her killed. She also adds that it has been thirty days since she has even seen the king (**4:11**). As a side note, this shows us that even being queen wasn't a great life. She had no closeness with her husband and had no right to see him unless HE wanted it. If he went thirty days without even caring to see her, I highly doubt fidelity was part of the equation.

After her fearful response, Mordecai reminds her that she is not likely to escape the edict to kill all Jews just because she is a queen, pointing out that she has nothing really to lose by asking the king for mercy. He then shows great faith and tells her that God is going to deliver HIS people one way or another, so she can either be part of the problem or part of the solution. He declares that this critical time might be the whole reason God has allowed her to come to the position of queen! (**4:12-14**)

In the end, Esther showed her great faith. She may have needed a little motivation from someone who had more faith when she was struggling, but that's true for all of us. When she agreed to go to the king and put her trust in the Lord, she told Mordecai, "If I perish, I perish" (**4:16**). Esther and Mordecai were both willing to give up their very lives for the cause of standing up for God's people, and they trusted that whatever happened would be the Lord's will.

You can read the rest of the story to see how God thwarts the plans of the wicked and saves His people through the strength and faith of Esther, who literally put her life on the line. God's name is never mentioned in the book of Esther, but He is working behind the scenes throughout it.

The same is true in your life. You may feel like He has allowed so much tragedy, abuse, and brokenness in your life. You may feel like He has weakened you. But if you trust Him and live in that faith, you'll see and know that He is still at work to use everything that has been done to bring His plan to fruition. God is always in control!

Chapter 32
The Faith of Hannah

Have you ever wanted something that you couldn't have so badly that it made you literally sick? If so, then you know how difficult it is to even focus on anything else in life. You can't be happy for anyone else. In fact, if another person is enjoying the blessing you so desperately crave, you'll most likely resent him or her. You also can't enjoy any of the blessings you ARE receiving in life because all you can think about is the thing that you wish you could have. An attitude of dissatisfaction can steal all of your joy and some of the joy from others as well.

Sometimes, God keeps us from getting what we want because he knows we need to get our priorities straight first. We need HIM to be what we desire most and for all other wants or needs that we have to be submitted to Him. God may eventually give us the thing for which we are desperate, but waiting for it allows us to practice trusting in Him, to be willing to submit all of our desires to Him, and to appreciate the blessing all the more if/when we do get it. This is exactly what happened with Hannah, who went from being barren to birthing one of the most steadfast, bold, and faithful men who I've already discussed in this book - Samuel.

I've decided to double-dip on the phrase in **Hebrews 11:34** that says there were some "whose weakness was turned to strength" because of their faith. I talked about the faith and story of Esther in the last chapter, but it seems to me I'd be doing a disservice to this entire book of faithful heroes if I didn't talk about Hannah. It just so happens that, like Esther, Hannah was one who was in a position of weakness, but through her trust in God and desire to obey Him, she became strong and faithful.

The story is found in **1 Samuel 1** and I encourage you to read the whole thing even as I give you the bullet points. We are first told about this man, Elkanah, who had two wives named Hannah and Peninnah (**v. 2**). It's important for us to understand the fact that even though polygamy was somewhat of a norm in ancient Israel, it doesn't mean that God accepted it. The Bible never puts polygamy in a positive light. It tells us that God brought together one man and one woman at the beginning of human life (**Genesis 2:21-24**). It's very possible that polygamy, like many sins that we have today, became so culturally accepted to the point that participants were ignorant of the fact that it wasn't good. But all we have to do is look at the tension, stress, and bitterness that it causes to see that it certainly was not part of God's intended plan.

The two wives of Elkanah developed a rivalry between them (**vv. 6-7**). Peninnah was given children, but the Lord had closed Hannah's womb. Since motherhood is such a high honor and was back then as well, it seems that Peninnah used this to provoke Hannah. In the constant competition for their husband's love and attention, Peninnah had the upper hand and both she and Hannah knew it. That didn't stop Elkanah from loving Hannah. In fact, he would give her a double portion of the meat whenever they worshiped and sacrificed to the Lord each year at Shiloh because he loved her and knew that she was distraught over not having children (**vv. 3-5**). Elkanah, like many men, did his best to love his wife but simply couldn't understand how she felt. He was loving but insensitive and failed to see that what she desperately needed was something that he could not provide unless the Lord chose to allow it.

Hannah was so distraught over her situation and cried so much that she wouldn't even eat. Then one time, after her family had finished eating, she got up and began to pray "in deep anguish" and with "bitter weeping" (**v. 10**). In that prayer, Hannah made a vow to the Lord that if He cared about her misery enough to give her a son, then she would "give him to the Lord for all the days of his life, and no razor would ever be used on his head" (**v. 11**). This was a Nazirite vow, the same one commanded by the Lord regarding Samson's birth in **Judges 13:2-5**.

A Nazirite vow was similar to something you and I might do for Lent or for an even longer period of time. It was traditionally done for a season in ancient Israel, but as far as I know, Samson and Samuel are the only ones who were considered Nazirites from birth. Maybe that type of submission to His will was just what God wanted to see before he chose to bless her. Hannah did the right thing in taking her feelings of grief and anguish to the Lord rather than trying to meet her needs through other means.

After spending time in prayer and pouring her heart and desires out to the Lord, she is initially reprimanded by the priest because he thinks she is just drunk. But after she explains what she is doing, the priest sends her away with an encouragement and a blessing (**vv. 12-17**). When we pour ourselves out to the Lord in desperation, He often gives us little nuggets of hope through others before the blessing comes. We see this happen between Hannah and the priest because, after he encourages her, she finds the strength to eat something (**v. 18**). That strength continues the next day as she gets up and worships the Lord before going home.

I remind you that she does this AFTER submitting her desire to the Lord but BEFORE she knows how or even if He will respond. Our worship of the Lord is about who He is, not what He does for us. If we think about all He has done for us, we should always worship Him anyway. But if we base it on that alone, we tend to start focusing on what God HASN'T done for us and begin to think He isn't worthy of our worship. Hannah learned to praise Him no matter what.

After they went home, Hannah and Elkanah slept together as they probably had done many times before, but this time the Lord remembered her and she became pregnant with Samuel (**v. 20**). It probably would have been tempting at that point to thank God for the gift and then hold onto it and neglect the vow she had made. Anyone who has had children and has had to let them go at some point knows this to be true. But Hannah faithfully follows through on her promise and presents Samuel to the priest at the Lord's house in Shiloh after he is weaned (**vv. 21-28**).

Hannah's life was in the dumps. Not only did she not get what she wanted in terms of a child at first, but her husband had another wife right there in the same home who got what Hannah wanted and rubbed it in on occasion. Her deep anguish didn't lead her away from the Lord, however, but right to Him. Rather than respond to Peninnah's provoking behavior, she went to the Lord. Rather than stop believing, she went to the Lord. Rather than engage in other immoral behavior to meet her needs, she went to the Lord. Because of this, she became a woman of great faith and strength, and she gave the Lord all the credit. In **1 Samuel 2:1**, she says, "In the Lord my horn is lifted high." The word for "horn" is the Hebrew *carni*, which is a figurative symbol of strength.

Hannah trusted in God and He turned what was a great weakness for her into a great strength as she gave birth to a man who led Israel with truth and grace. What can God do in your life if you trust Him with your most desperate needs and deepest sorrows? You may feel weak, but depending on Him will make you strong and faithful.

CHAPTER 33
THE FAITH OF JEHOSHAPHAT

In 2005, Hurricane Katrina ravaged the Gulf Coast and even the inland parts of multiple southern states. Many of those places were hit hard again several weeks later when Hurricane Rita made an appearance. As many know, the biggest city that was impacted to the point it was almost completely under water during these events was New Orleans, Louisiana. As a response to the devastation that was occurring in her state, then-Louisiana governor Kathleen Blanco made a statement where she called on Louisianans and all people everywhere to pray for those affected and for their state.

At the time, I often listened to sports talk radio as I drove around in my work vehicle all day and one host in particular was Colin Cowherd. He is still someone I enjoy listening to, but he decided one day to comment on Governor Blanco's plea for prayers in a way that showed his ignorance toward the things of God. His response was something to the effect of saying that the people of Louisiana elected her to come up with something better than prayer. He was dumbfounded that asking for prayer was the best solution she could come up with and declared that she was not fit to lead and handle this crisis.

While I can understand that many use prayer as a substitute for action and that doing so is not necessarily the point of faith in God, Colin Cowherd simply failed to see any power in seeking the Lord during a crisis. As we continue to look at the heroes of our faith in this book, we find out that most of these people were eyewitnesses to the power of God long after they had run out of human options and plans to save them from their crises. King (don't call him "Jumpin") Jehoshaphat was no different.

In **Hebrews 11:34**, we're told that some of the faithful heroes "became powerful in battle and routed foreign armies" through their trust in the Lord. This achievement could be applied to many of the heroes, but Jehoshaphat is certainly near the top of that list.

His story is found in **2 Chronicles 17-20** after he succeeds his father Asa as king of Judah. In **2 Chronicles 17:3-6**, we see that Jehoshaphat followed the Lord and the ways of his ancestor, David, and that he did away with idols and their symbols and refused to consult them. The Lord chose to establish his kingdom and He gave great wealth and honor to Jehoshaphat. **Verse 9** tells us that he also appointed teachers to go throughout Judah teaching the Book of the Law of the Lord. In other words, he didn't just do away with idol worship, but also replaced it with a renewed national focus on the Lord. As Jehoshaphat made good choices and kept his focus on the things of God, he grew more and more powerful, and other kings surrounding Judah were afraid of him to the point that they brought gifts, likely to get on his good side.

In **2 Chronicles 18**, Jehoshaphat almost falls into a trap set by the evil King Ahab of Israel. He does make the mistake of allying himself with Ahab by marriage first, but then agrees to join him in war (**vv. 1-3**). However, he urges Ahab to seek the counsel of the Lord first (**v. 4**). Ahab, probably somewhat begrudgingly, calls on all the prophets at his disposal and asks them if he should go to war specifically against Ramoth Gilead. They all tell him how awesome he is and that he should do it and will have victory. I say he probably consulted them begrudgingly for several reasons. First, he has shown little to no regard for the word of the Lord at any time during his reign up to this point. Second, his actions in the rest of the chapter show that he didn't care much for it at this point either! Peer pressure can be a good thing in the Church, and it seems to me that Jehoshaphat put the pressure on Ahab to seek the Lord if he truly wanted Jehoshaphat's help.

Ahab had 400 prophets who just told him the good news he wanted to hear and didn't speak the Lord's true word if it meant bad news for Ahab. Jehoshaphat caught onto this and asked, "Is there no longer a prophet of the Lord here whom we can inquire of?" (**v. 6**) Ahab responds that there is still Micaiah, but he hates him because everything Micaiah usually prophesies is bad news for him. Both Jehoshaphat's question and Ahab's response reveal that BOTH men recognized that the 400 "yes-men" were not true prophets but only gave lip service. The difference is that the Lord's word truly mattered to Jehoshaphat, while Ahab was content to, as Paul later says in **2 Timothy 4:3**, surround himself with those who said what his "itching ears wanted to hear."

They talk to Micaiah and true to form, Micaiah prophesies the bad news that Ahab predicted. Ahab would be deceived into thinking he could win the battle but instead would be killed. Hearing all this, Ahab continues to get further away from the Lord spiritually and tries to use all the resources available to him to save himself. He puts Micaiah in prison until he returns safely, as if Micaiah is the one who had the power to doom him. He then tries to get Jehoshaphat to stand out in battle so he would be killed while Ahab disguised himself. Jehoshaphat realizes he has been duped after it's too late and he's about to be killed, but **2 Chronicles 18:31** tells us he cries out to the Lord in that moment of crisis and God rescues him. Ahab would later be killed "at random" (**v. 33**) and the prophecy was fulfilled.

In **2 Chronicles 19**, Jehoshaphat returns from battle, is held accountable by a seer named Jehu for joining forces with the wicked Ahab, then returns to seeking the Lord completely. He appoints judges throughout Judah and urges them to judge carefully because they are judging for the Lord and not for mere mortals (**vv. 5-7**). In **2 Chronicles 20**, we see the climax of Jehoshaphat's story. He is told that a vast army made up of the Moabites, Ammonites, and Meunites is coming to wage war against him and God's people (**v. 1**). Any one of these groups alone would have been a tall task to defeat. This would be like the three best NFL teams all coming together to take on the Cleveland Browns! Jehoshaphat doesn't panic and he doesn't spend a lot of time coming up with a "plan" to win like Ahab did. Instead, he stands up before all the people of Judah and begins to pray to God, reminding Him of His awesomeness and power, reminding Him of what He's promised and what He's done in the past, and acknowledging that they are in trouble and need the Lord to show up (**vv. 5-11**). He finishes with these great words in **verse 12**: "Our God, will you not judge them? For we have no power to face this vast army that is attacking us. We do not know what to do, but our eyes are on you."

Friends, that's the essence of humility before the Lord and admitting you need Him during a crisis. It could be an army attacking your nation, a natural disaster destroying your home and everything you've worked for, or something that hits even closer to home like battling addiction or losing your job. Whatever crisis is facing you, there is power in prayer and in sincerely giving it all over to God. He has the power to win the battle FOR you, so that all you need to do is whatever little bit He tells you.

Read the rest of **2 Chronicles 20** on your own and see how the Lord delivered Jehoshaphat and the people of Judah without them having to lift a single sword or kill a single soul. All they had to do was trust the Lord, put their faith in action by marching against their enemies while praising God with a song we still sing today - "Give thanks to the Lord, for his love endures forever" (**v. 21**) - and then gather the plunder the Lord had given them after He used the pagan armies to literally destroy each other. God almost always calls us to ACT out of our faith and trust in Him, but even then the battle belongs to HIM. Stop trusting in your plans and efforts today and seek the Lord with all your heart!

CHAPTER 34
THE FAITH OF THE WIDOW AT ZAREPHATH

We've all heard that actions speak louder than words. I can preach a good sermon and talk for 30-40 minutes straight and people might even say I'm a good preacher, but that won't go very far in determining what they think of me as a Christian. In fact, for Christians, the better thing to say would be that actions speak louder than "beliefs." Many of us know what we're supposed to believe as Christians and we even know how to talk the talk. But even Jesus said that not everyone who calls him "Lord" will enter the kingdom of heaven, but only the one who DOES the will of the Father (**Matthew 7:21** [caps mine]). The Church is in an age when an increasing number of so-called "believers" either show no evidence of their stated faith or boldly show evidence that contradicts it.

Continuing in the stories of the heroes of our faith shows us individuals who did more than just talk about what they believed. In many cases, they didn't talk about it at all and in other cases, they weren't even considered part of God's people until the acts of faith for which they are now known. In **Hebrews 11:35**, the writer continues to tell about the faithful anonymous, reminding us that "women received back their dead, raised to life again." There are only a couple people from the Old Testament who would fit this description, and the one I will address this chapter wasn't just anonymous to the writer of Hebrews, but also to whoever recorded her story in the first place. She is known as the widow at Zarephath and her story is found in the midst of Elijah's story in **1 Kings 17:7-24**.

The faith of Elijah and that of the widow are intertwined during a desperate time for both of them. Elijah has been on the run ever since he decided to confront King Ahab and his evil wife, Jezebel. God sends him to the middle of the wilderness and far away from any civilization where Ahab could possibly locate him, and he lives daily by depending on a brook for water and ravens who have been directed by God to bring him food. His faith is strong as he depends on God daily for his needs and doesn't worry about the next day. But then, God decides it's time for another move, which means another huge step of faith.

The brook, Elijah's one source of water, dries up, and God tells him to go to Zarephath in the region of Sidon because God has directed a widow in that place to supply Elijah with food (**v. 9**). Now, what we need to understand is that widows in those times were considered to be extremely poor because they had lost their source of income when their husbands had passed away. To Elijah, it probably made more sense for him to wait beside the dry brook and see what happens. When God calls us to move on, however, we can try to depend on the past and get the blessing back as much as we want and it still won't change God's mind.

God clearly had a plan to not only grow Elijah's faith, but to bring this desperate widow to faith and knowledge of Him. That's often how it works. You might complain about your circumstances to the Lord, but they may not change because He may want to use the testing of your faith as an example to someone who doesn't know Him. Elijah goes to the widow as directed and he finds her gathering sticks at the town gate (**v. 10**). Elijah was probably hoping he would find that this widow was unusually rich, but what he found in reality is that she was even poorer than most widows. She didn't even have firewood! After Elijah asks her to bring him water and a piece of bread, she declares that she has no bread and that she is gathering the sticks just so that she and her son can enjoy one last meal before they starve to death (**v. 12**).

At this point, Elijah has learned not to pay any attention to his circumstances when he knows what God's word is and he is ready to live out his faith in front of the widow. He tells her not to be afraid because the God of Israel has promised that her oil and flour, the last resources she has available to her, will not be used up until the Lord sends rain on the land (**v. 14**). There had been no rain in the land because of Ahab's wickedness and the lack of rain ultimately led to a great famine, which made the situation even more desperate for people like the widow. Yet, despite all of this,

Elijah declared that God would miraculously meet her needs if she just trusts in Him.

That's a big "if," for the widow at Zarephath and for all of us. God wants to bless us and we may "say" what we think we're supposed to say to try to get the blessing, but our actions always speak louder than words when it comes to faith. Elijah boldly told the woman that she could make food for herself and her son, but the way she would show trust in the God of Israel would be by making a small loaf of bread for Elijah FIRST (**v. 13**). What if Elijah was wrong? What if he was selfishly taking advantage of a poor woman? Sometimes, God calls us to do things that will lead to us being misunderstood. But again, true faith trusts God with even those concerns. He can handle meeting daily food needs and He can definitely handle our reputations.

The woman has a choice to make. God is ready to bless her and Elijah knows it, but neither one of them is going to force her to LIVE her faith in this situation. The connection to our faithful choices and eventual blessing are all throughout Scripture. The blessing may not always look like prosperity, and the widow did not get rich off of her faith. But she did get her daily needs met. She did exactly as Elijah, who had spoken the word of the Lord, told her (**v. 15**), and she learned to put her full faith in the true God of Israel who could and would meet her daily needs.

The rest of the chapter tells us that her son would later get sick, so sick in fact that he stops breathing (**v. 17**). She assumes maybe Elijah has caused this but then immediately begins to look at her own sin as a possible reason. Elijah takes the boy and cries out to the Lord on his behalf, reminding God that the widow does not deserve this because she was very poor, trusted and followed Him, and even continued to allow Elijah to stay with her. Elijah questions whether God would bring this tragedy on her and **verse 22** tells us that God heard Elijah's cry and allowed the boy's life to return to him. The end result in **verse 24** is that the widow at Zarephath states that she knows Elijah is a man of God and, more importantly, that the word of the Lord that flows through Elijah's mouth is the "truth."

The widow learned that even in her most desperate circumstances, faith was about her actions and not words. She probably figured she had nothing to lose with the food. Whether you eat one more meal and die or eat no more meals and die, what's the big difference? So, she did what God commanded through Elijah and received the blessing that came from it. But when it came to her son, she had everything to lose. Yet, she turned to the Lord then. Her newfound faith as a Gentile woman taught her that this God was real, and that His power could meet all of her needs and fix any situation if He wanted it to. When she put her full faith in God and His servant Elijah, she received her son back to life even after he had been dead.

The same can be true for you. I don't know what you're facing now in your life, but I do know that it's there because God is giving you an opportunity to put your faith in Him beyond your words and into your actions.

CHAPTER 35
THE FAITH OF THE APOSTLE PAUL

In the past, I had a conversation with a man from my church about how every day there are examples of the reality that life is all about choices. We see that **Deuteronomy 30:15** says, "See, I set before you today life and prosperity, death and destruction." The Lord has been basically telling the Israelites through Moses that this isn't rocket science. The choices are clear and each person must make their decision regarding what they really want.

The man from my church was telling me that he had an opportunity to begin to teach his 5-year-old son about this. They went to a baseball game for the local independent league professional team and were sitting in the grass just beyond the fence. As they were watching, a home run was hit and landed very close to them. The little boy got excited and told his dad he wanted to get a home run ball. As they continued to pay attention waiting for the next one, the little boy looked over and saw a playground nearby. He wanted to go play with other children, so he asked his dad if he could. His dad reminded him that he wanted a home run ball and said that if he goes to the playground, he won't be there to catch a ball if it's hit there. The boy asked when the home run ball is going to come and his dad said he doesn't know and it might not happen either way, but that the boy would have to choose which fun thing matters more to him.

In **Hebrews 11:35**, we see that some of the anonymously faithful also faced a choice, and some "were tortured, refusing to be released so that they might gain an even better resurrection." The idea of it being a better resurrection pertains to the beginning of the verse, which was discussed in the previous chapter, about "women who received back their dead, raised to life again." The writer is reminding believers that while those women had faith and received the joy of their loved ones being raised back to life, those individuals merely returned to a hurting, broken, and imperfect world. The writer explains that those who endured torture all the way to death will receive a resurrection that is "better" because it takes us to glory. It is a permanent and perfect resurrection.

Now, I have to say that this particular description of faithful heroes presents a problem because there is no specific story from the Old Testament that seems to directly correlate to what the writer of Hebrews is describing. We have to remember that there were other writings besides the books of the Bible that were not considered to be part of the Biblical canon but were likely known to many of the educated Jews. Two such books would be 1 and 2 Maccabees, and it appears that 2 Maccabees is where we would find the story of a scribe named Eleazar and the torture he endured. Scholars seem to agree that Eleazar's story is what the writer of Hebrews was referencing in this description. There's no doubt in my mind that the writer of Hebrews, whether it was Paul, Peter, or some other educated Jew, knew of the story of Eleazar. That being said, I have no idea whether scholars are right or wrong, so I'm going to veer off the beaten path a bit on this one and talk about someone from the New Testament that fits this description.

When considering who might be the author of Hebrews, many traditionally believed it was Paul, but more recently people have agreed that only God can truly know. Of all the possibilities that scholars have thrown out there, it seems clear that if it wasn't Paul, it was someone who knew him very well. My personal Bible happens to be the Men's Devotional Bible from Zondervan and it specifically lists the approximate dates that each book was written. This is certainly not an exact science, but it's worth noting that 2 Corinthians is said to have been written around 55 AD, while the book of Hebrews is said to have been written 10-15 years after that. If it was written by either Paul or someone who knew him, it stands to reason that they could have had Paul's torture in mind even if they weren't directly describing his faith in the way they described Eleazar's.

In **2 Corinthians 11:23-26**, Paul explains some of the tortures he experienced because of his faith in Christ. He states that he was imprisoned, severely flogged, beaten with rods, pelted with stones, and constantly in danger because of those who were dead set on killing him. He specifically says, "Five times I received from the

Jews the forty lashes minus one" (**v. 24**). This is a reference to some of the most cruel torture ever invented. The Jews believed that 40 lashes would kill any person, so the way to exact the most pain on a person without killing them (though at times someone would die well before the 40th lash) was to whip them 1 time less than what would kill them. Paul lived his life for the cause of Christ and to share the good news of Jesus with everyone he could. He didn't worry about death or pain. In fact, some of his letters lead you to believe that he frankly couldn't wait for death!

Paul was assured of the glory and resurrection that awaited him after his very temporary suffering and torture in this world came to an end. He wrote, "For to me, to live is Christ and to die is gain" (**Philippians 1:21**). He also spoke to his friends and elders in Ephesus, knowing it would be the last time he would see them, before he went to Jerusalem: "I only know that in every city the Holy Spirit warns me that prison and hardships are facing me. However, I consider my life worth nothing to me; my only aim is to finish the race and complete the task the Lord Jesus has given me - the task of testifying to the good news of God's grace" (**Acts 20:23-24**). Earlier, in **Acts 16**, Paul and his ministry partner Silas had been unfairly thrown into prison after being "severely flogged," then refused to leave the prison even after it appeared that God had supernaturally opened the doors for them to do so. Because they stuck around, the jailer who was seconds away from killing himself came to know Jesus along with his entire family and they were all saved and baptized (**vv. 26-34**).

Paul had many opportunities to choose what was easier at the time. He could choose to follow Jesus fully, knowing it would lead to great suffering temporarily in this world but believing in the "better resurrection," or he could choose to walk away from that task Jesus had given him and take an easier worldly road.

You and I face the same choice regularly. Knowing Jesus means you have to do away with sins of comfort and follow Him even when it isn't easy. It means you may face suffering from resisting temptation and eventually may receive it in the way of persecution. But the knowledge that this is all temporary and that someday we'll be in paradise with Jesus just like the thief who suffered tremendous pain right next to Him on the cross motivates us to endure anything we face on this earth. Make the right choice today, then make it again tomorrow. Pretty soon, it'll be a habit and, like Paul, you'll live in true freedom!

Jeremiah / *Jeremiah 20:9*
"His word is in my heart like a fire,
a fire shut up in my bones.
I am weary of holding it in;
indeed, I cannot."

Chapter 36
The Faith of Jeremiah

Have you ever stopped and reflected on your life and wondered how in the world you ended up where you are? This can happen in either a very positive or a very negative light. Personally, I've had those moments when I found myself leading a church in Marion, Ohio or ministering to the homeless in Findlay, Ohio after spending the first twenty-seven years of my life in Pennsylvania. As of the printing of this book, I'm living back in Pennsylvania, residing and ministering in a town forty minutes from where I grew up yet still very familiar to me because of the four years that God allowed me to earn an income as a driver for FedEx Ground here. I'm experiencing all of this with my wife who "just happened" to wind up in Ohio at the same time I was and "just happened" to get a job at the homeless shelter where I was working, even though she spent most of her life growing up in Virginia. When I look back on my life, I realize not much of it could have been predicted and most of it is an example of God's grace, His providence, and His GOOD plan.

Most of you could probably say the same thing about your own lives and the directions they have taken. We don't always realize that God is working when He is, but it's fairly easy to see when we take a moment to reflect on our lives. However, the question I shared above can also be asked when we find ourselves in the midst of negative circumstances. I can think of very specific times in my life when I looked around at the destruction and misery that surrounded me as a result of my own choices and wondered how I could have ever gotten that far down the wrong path. Again, I'm sure many of you reading this could say you've had those moments as well. The results in our lives can often be traced back to either God's goodness or our own sins.

What we should know as believers in the Lord is that when we follow Him, it's a dangerous thing to evaluate our decisions and lives solely on our circumstances. While "reaping what you sow" is generally a true concept and is even Biblical (**Galatians 6:7**), the reaping doesn't always make sense to our finite minds and worldly ways of examining our circumstances. One thing we've seen through this look at the heroes of our faith is that God sometimes blesses them even when they are caught in sin and allows them to suffer when they appear to be following Him wholeheartedly. God uses everything according to His will and sometimes we don't reap the rewards of our faith until we spend eternity with Him.

One faithful hero who likely often wondered how he could end up where he did was the prophet Jeremiah. Despite his faithfulness to God, he was known as "the weeping prophet" and rarely reaped any positive consequences from his obedient sowing. More than just mental anguish over the state of his people, he also experienced great physical and emotional torment. **Hebrews 11:36** tells us that some of the anonymously faithful "faced jeers and flogging," which could probably be characterized today as severe verbal and physical abuse. Jeremiah was one of several people from the Old Testament who would likely fit this description.

In **Jeremiah 20**, we see that a priest named Pashhur, who at the time was the official in charge of the temple of the Lord, has Jeremiah "beaten and put in stocks" because he was upset about the things Jeremiah was preaching regarding the Lord's anger toward the sins of the nation (**vv. 1-2**). A commentary I was reading from Enduring Word suggests that the expression translated as "beaten" most likely referred to the "forty lashes minus one" concept applied during a severe flogging. You may remember that the Apostle Paul experienced this most painful of beatings five times. In addition, the "stocks" refers to a structure in which a prisoner was locked into a twisted and confined position to cause increasing pain and discomfort. By the way, this was likely AFTER he had already been flogged. So, it's not like his wounds were healed before his body was forcefully contorted. **Verse 3** tells us that Jeremiah was released the next day, which means he was kept in that position for the rest of the day!

This didn't stop Jeremiah from continuing to speak whatever the Lord commanded him to speak. He was a prophet of the Lord and was not willing to water down the message in order to make people happy and save himself from harm. Jeremiah would face many other obstacles and extreme punishments during his time as a prophet, including being thrown in prison in **Jeremiah 37** and then lowered into a cistern with no water and only mud in **Jeremiah 38**. That last punishment was intended to kill him; he was done. **Jeremiah 38:6** says that he "sank down into the mud." If those aren't the cruelest of circumstances for someone who has done nothing but obey God, I don't know what is. He was literally sinking into the mud in a cistern deep in the ground with no way to save himself or meet any of his other needs. He would die by either suffocation in the mud or starvation, whichever happened first.

God moved in the heart of one of the officials to rescue him before it was too late, but Jeremiah was certainly aware of how much pain had come to his life because he was obedient. There is a section in the book that specifically lays out Jeremiah's complaint to God. It's found in **Jeremiah 20:7-18** and I encourage you to read it yourself. At first glance, it may come across like he is deranged and literally going back and forth between worship and whining. But such is the life of one who obeys the Lord in the face of intense opposition and endures all of the pain that comes with it.

He says he is "ridiculed all day long" and mocked by everyone (**v. 7**). He adds, "The word of the Lord has brought me insult and reproach all day long" (**v. 8**). We already know about his being beaten/flogged. He reflects on his life and has the thoughts most of us would: "Why did I ever come out of the womb to see trouble and sorrow and to end my days in shame?" (**v. 18**) Yet, even in the midst of all the pain and suffering he faced, Jeremiah reminds himself that he was born to be the very prophet of the Lord that he was: "But if I say, 'I will not mention his word or speak anymore in his name,' his word is in my heart like a fire, a fire shut up in my bones. I am weary of holding it in; indeed, I cannot" (**v. 9**). This is portrayed in the artwork just before this chapter.

Jeremiah knew what he was born to do (God told him in **Jeremiah 1:5** that He knew him BEFORE he was even born and that He had appointed him as a prophet to the nations) and the thought of not doing it was worse than enduring the pain and suffering that came because he was obedient to the Lord. This is a faithful hero if I ever read about one. He may have faced jeers and flogging, but his obedience forced the people who should have been honoring God all along to have to face their own wickedness. While they ultimately did not listen to Jeremiah and were overtaken by the Babylonians as a result, Jeremiah could rest knowing that he did everything he could to stop it.

Are you willing to speak the truth of God's word to others no matter what it causes to take place in your life? People may not listen to you, but that's between them and God. What you share and how you represent God's word to them is between YOU and God. You may not reap good circumstances for yourself in this lifetime, but trust in God as your full reward and reap the benefits for all of eternity.

CHAPTER 37
THE FAITH OF MICAIAH

Without a doubt, one of the most iconic movie scenes in history comes from *A Few Good Men*. Even if you haven't seen it, you probably know the scene. Lieutenant Daniel Kaffee, the attorney played by Tom Cruise, has the brazen, corrupt Colonel Nathan R. Jessup, played by Jack Nicholson, on the witness stand as he tries to get to the bottom of what took place that led to the death of a young Marine stationed in Cuba under Jessup's command. As they go back and forth playing their legal "games," the conversation escalates to Lt. Kaffee emphatically demanding the truth. Colonel Jessup screams back, "You can't handle the truth!" Jessup goes on to express his displeasure with those who enjoy the freedom he provides but constantly question the manner in which he provides it.

There is some truth in Jessup's words. We gather for fun on holidays that are supposed to honor military service or celebrate freedoms several times each year, but we may not really stop and remember the sacrifices of those who have given everything in order to provide us with the freedom we enjoy year-round, and sometimes we even question our military's decisions. As I personally think about those who have given their lives for me, the list of course starts with Jesus but includes so many whose names I'll never even know. Those men and women were willing to run toward danger and do jobs that so many others are unwilling to do. They deserve to be called "heroes" because they stood up to fear when so many others could not or would not. Some of them even experienced opposition from their own countrymen as those who opposed military action hurled their insults and frustrations directly at the soldiers who were just trying to serve their nation. They are heroes because they went against the grain.

The heroes of our faith that we've been reviewing in this book ought to be seen the same way. What made them stand out in most cases was their willingness to go against the grain, against what was popular, or even against what was comfortable in order to be counted as faithful and obedient to the Lord and His will.

In this chapter, we look at a man who was briefly mentioned in the chapter on Jehoshaphat earlier in this book. **Hebrews 11:36** says that some of the anonymously faithful faced "chains and imprisonment." This might not seem like it's as harrowing as what so many others went through. I've been in multiple prisons doing ministry in my life and I've yet to see someone being tortured or even greatly mistreated. I'm not saying it doesn't happen, but we have to understand that what we know as imprisonment today in our country is far from what it was like for those who were hated during Biblical times.

One man who suffered greatly and was imprisoned for following the Lord and going against what was popular was the prophet Micaiah. We don't know a lot about him since his presence in the Bible is short-lived, but we do know that he was faithful and bold. His story is part of the story of the evil King Ahab of Israel and King Jehoshaphat of Judah. It is found in multiple places, but I'll be looking at the account in **2 Chronicles 18**.

King Ahab wanted to go to war and capture a city called Ramoth Gilead, but he wanted King Jehoshaphat to join forces and help him. Jehoshaphat wouldn't do it unless Ahab first sought the counsel of the Lord (**2 Chronicles 18:4**). Ahab then summoned four hundred men who all said that God would give the city into Ahab's hand. This somehow prompted Jehoshaphat to ask if there were any ACTUAL prophets of the Lord whom they could ask. Something about the way those four hundred men carried themselves made it somewhat obvious that they were merely "yes" men who couldn't have cared less what God was actually saying. Maybe they were scared of what the king would do if they gave him bad news (we'll see in a bit why they had reason for this fear). Maybe they had originally been true prophets but had abandoned the Lord in order to do what was popular.

Ahab told Jehoshaphat that the one prophet left through whom they could inquire of the Lord was Micaiah, but Ahab admitted right off the bat that he hated Micaiah because he only prophesies bad things about Ahab. This shows us what Micaiah was known for. Four hundred other "prophets" were known for saying whatever pleased the evil king. But one man went against the grain and was known for speaking the truth about an evil man who disobeyed the Lord.

It's not that he had it out for Ahab. Prophecy is not always a mystery. If a man does bad things, worships idols, marries a foreign woman who makes it her mission to murder prophets of the Lord, and continues to reject God completely, how can any prophet worth his salt suggest that such a man has a bright future and will be blessed by God? Micaiah was simply the only one who was willing to say what was TRUE.

When Ahab sent for him, Micaiah was brought out by officials. This, combined with his RETURN to the officials at the end of the story in **verse 25**, reveals that Micaiah was most likely already in prison before he was summoned by Ahab. It's no wonder so many of the other prophets were afraid to deliver bad news to Ahab. If he didn't like what you said, he just sent you off to prison until he felt like letting you go. As Micaiah is summoned, Ahab's messenger urges him to prophesy in agreement with the other four hundred, but Micaiah declares that he can only speak as the Lord directs (**vv. 12-13**). It was preposterous in his eyes to think that a mere man can change or control the words of the immortal God. It wasn't even about what Micaiah desired. I'm sure he desired to say something that pleased the king so that his own suffering would end, but he didn't even see that as an option.

Micaiah's first response to Ahab was, "Attack and be victorious," but Ahab reminded him that he wanted the truth (**vv. 14-15**). This tells us that Micaiah's initial response was likely very sarcastic. Something about it told Ahab that he wasn't being serious. It's ironic that Ahab demanded the truth because he had shown for his entire reign as king that he couldn't handle it!

Micaiah could have channeled his inner-Jessup and blasted Ahab for demanding something that he couldn't accept deep down in places he doesn't talk about at parties. Instead, Micaiah just went right back to speaking the hard truth he always did and declared that Ahab would be killed when he went into battle. Another prophet, Zedekiah, slapped Micaiah in the face, because when you can't handle the truth, you resort to violence. Ahab then ordered Micaiah back to prison and ordered that he be given only bread and water until Ahab would return safely (**vv. 25-26**). The NKJV of this passage calls it "the bread and water of affliction," which basically meant that Micaiah would be stuck in prison and only receiving the bare essentials for the rest of his life.

Ahab's real problem was with God, yet he couldn't do anything to get back at God so he took out his frustrations on God's true servant. Micaiah never wavered in his resolve to be faithful and obedient to God. He responded to Ahab that if he were to ever return safely, that would mean the Lord had not spoken through Micaiah at all (**v. 27**). Micaiah didn't worry about the circumstances he faced. He stood his ground on the truth of the Lord's word and was willing to be judged by whether the prophecy was fulfilled rather than the popular opinion of man. Ahab wanted to inflict as much suffering on Micaiah as he could without killing him, and I know of no evidence that Micaiah ever got out of prison. But the prophecy came true and Ahab was killed in the battle for Ramoth Gilead.

Micaiah wasn't hailed as a hero among his peers, but he certainly was a hero of the faith. As you are reminded of his story, as well as so many others who heroically stood up against evil and went against the grain, be one who is obedient and true to the Lord regardless of personal cost. Be bold. Be courageous. Be a hero.

Chapter 38
The Faith of Zechariah

What kind of legacy are you leaving for those who will come after you? This question is one that haunts some people as they near the end of their lives and causes many others to make changes when they consider it early enough in their time on this earth. It's why so many young couples show little or no interest in church until they have children and begin to think about how it would be good for their little ones, even if they still don't follow Jesus themselves as adults. It's also why those same adults have no problem with colorful language until their children begin to repeat after them, at which point they shudder at the thought of the example they are setting!

There's a great Christian song in country music called "Three Wooden Crosses." The song is about a terrible traffic accident in which 3 out of 4 people riding on a bus are killed. Three wooden crosses are eventually put up on the side of the highway and the singer says he doesn't know why there isn't four there. It turns out the four individuals were a farmer, a teacher, a preacher, and a prostitute. The song tells us that it's not what we take with us when we leave this world that's important, but what we leave behind us when we go.

According to the song's lyrics, the farmer left a harvest, a home with 80 acres, and faith and love for growing things in his young son's heart. The teacher left her wisdom in the minds of her students. The preacher laid a blood-stained Bible in the prostitute's hand and asked her to look toward the promised land as she becomes the lone survivor of the accident. It turns out the singer is saying that his local preacher is the son of the prostitute, proving that the preacher who died in the accident left a legacy just like the farmer and teacher did, and his dying gift sent the prostitute on the road to Jesus and resulted in kingdom benefits for generations to come.

In this chapter, I want to briefly share the story of a faithful hero in the Bible who left a legacy with his dying words just like that preacher. In **Hebrews 11:37**, we're told that some of the past martyrs "were put to death by stoning." The man I want to tell you about this week, who was one of the Old Testament heroes murdered by stoning, was actually mentioned by name by Jesus. If you look at **Matthew 23:35**, Jesus is in the midst of pronouncing His woes on the Pharisees and teachers of the law. Here, He specifically mentions that blood will come upon them from the righteous blood that has been shed by previous martyrs, beginning with Abel and going all the way to Zechariah. A commentary by David Guzik says this is because Abel was the first faithful martyr (that makes sense since he is the first one mentioned in **Hebrews 11** and the first in this book) and Zechariah was the last one listed in the Hebrew Bible, which ended with 2 Chronicles.

Most scholars believe that Zechariah is the same man who was a prophet and wrote the book of Zechariah, but the story of his martyrdom is found in **2 Chronicles 24**. Zechariah, like many of the previous heroes we have discussed in this series, took center stage while so many others around him were wicked. After his father Berekiah (aka "Jehoiada"), a priest who was influential toward King Joash, passed away, Joash and the people of Judah turned away from the Lord and worshiped idols (**v. 18**). God tried to get their attention and get them back on track by sending prophets who proclaimed His word, but they refused to heed the warnings. One of those prophets was Zechariah and he once became bold in the Spirit, stood before everyone, and said, "This is what God says: 'Why do you disobey the Lord's commands? You will not prosper. Because you have forsaken the Lord, he has forsaken you'" (**v. 20**).

At that point, the people's reaction wasn't merely not listening to him in the sense of ignoring him. Rather than listen to the warning, repent, and plead with God to come back to them, they go the other direction. Their anger gets the best of them and they plot against Zechariah and even receive an order from King Joash to stone him to death in the courtyard of the temple (**v. 21**). It's somewhat shocking how quickly Joash could be willing to kill a man whose father had meant so much to him, but that just goes to show us how quickly sin can destroy us if we don't continue to repent and seek the Lord every day. But as Zechariah was dying, in his final moments he left a legacy statement: "May the Lord see this and call you to account" (**v. 22**).

Zechariah's statement comes off a little bit like he wants revenge on them. It doesn't exactly have the same ring to it that Stephen's plea for the Lord to not hold their sin against them as he was being stoned in **Acts 7:60** has. Yet, when Zechariah declares that he wants the Lord to call them to account, that doesn't necessarily mean he is asking for God to destroy them. The truth is we all have to give an account for our careless words and sins. There are only two ways we can give that account - we either experience the natural end result of our wickedness and die, or we trust in Jesus whose blood was "poured out for many for the forgiveness of sins" (**Matthew 26:28**). Zechariah understood that a savior was coming, and with his final words he pointed the people who murdered him toward that time when they would either pay for their sins themselves or trust in that savior.

Many Old Testament books talk about the savior who would come, and they present prophecies that would only be fulfilled by Jesus of Nazareth. Some of the clearest of these prophecies about Jesus are found in the book of Zechariah. He seemed to visualize what was going to happen to Jesus and how it would impact his own people. Toward the end of his book, Zechariah writes the word of the Lord about the death of the savior: "And I will pour out on the house of David and the inhabitants of Jerusalem a spirit of grace and supplication. They will look on me, the one they have pierced, and they will mourn for him as one mourns for an only child, and grieve bitterly for him as one grieves for a firstborn son" (**Zechariah 12:10**).

Zechariah's legacy as he lived and preached among the wicked was that he didn't hesitate to point them toward the One who is both Savior and righteous Judge. It ended up costing him his life, but that didn't stop him from proclaiming what the Lord had him proclaim. The One about whom he prophesied mentioned him along with all the other faithful martyrs. That's probably all we really need to know about Zechariah. Jesus Himself considered his spilt blood to be "righteous." I'd say that means he did something right in leaving a legacy for those after him.

What is your legacy? What would others say is most important to you? If you are spending time, money, and energy on something other than pointing people to Jesus, it's time to evaluate your priorities.

Chapter 39
The Faith of Isaiah

Having grown up in the 1990s, I consider the movie *Braveheart* a classic. *Braveheart* is the story of William Wallace, who led the Scottish revolt against the king of England beginning in the late 13th century. The theme of the movie is Wallace's quest for independence for his people in the face of the uncertainty of so many of his comrades, who at times boldly followed him and other times questioned his willingness to take on the establishment. During one conversation with his close friend and fellow rebel, Hamish, Wallace is considering taking the Scottish nobles up on their offer to join forces to go after the enemy. Hamish tries to convince Wallace that it's a trap (he would be proven correct on that), but Wallace is willing to take that chance because he knows it's the only way they could possibly achieve victory. Hamish, fearing the trap will lead to their gruesome torture and death, declares, "I don't want to be a martyr." Wallace responds, "Nor I. I want to live. I want a home, and children, and peace. I've asked God for these things. It's all for nothing if you don't have freedom."

Even after William Wallace was captured, he held true to the cause of freedom, refusing to confess his "crime" and swear allegiance to the king of England, even while being tortured and killed. He demonstrated that it is better to die fighting for what's right than live having accepted what is wrong. In **Hebrews 11:37**, we read about the unnamed heroes of the faith who experienced excruciating pain as they were martyred but never abandoned their allegiance to God. One of the descriptors is that "they were sawed in two." This is an interesting category of martyrs because we do not find any specific stories of someone being killed for their faith in this way anywhere in Scripture.

As I've found in doing some research, a theologian named John Gill explains in his exposition of the Bible that other historical Jewish texts, including the Talmud and the Midrash, have references to the death of Isaiah the prophet. These texts and Jewish tradition hold that Isaiah feared the evil King Manasseh, who took issue with some of his prophecies. Isaiah then ran away from the king and hid inside a cedar tree, but the outer edges of his clothing were visible and he was found. King Manasseh ordered that the tree be sawed in two while Isaiah was still in it, and this is how he was martyred.

Admittedly, I don't have copies of any of these historical texts in my possession, so I cannot verify their words. However, I do believe that **Hebrews 11** is true because, like the rest of Scripture, it is inspired by the very breath of God (**2 Timothy 3:16**). As the writer of Hebrews was putting pen to paper, we can be certain that the Holy Spirit was guiding him and that the Jews who would have read it would have been familiar with the tradition of Isaiah's martyrdom. But that's not all.

We can certainly look at the Scriptures that do describe this time in history and consider whether it's possible and even likely that King Manasseh might have killed Isaiah. **Isaiah 1:1** tells us that Isaiah was a prophet during the reigns of Uzziah, Jotham, Ahaz, and Hezekiah, who were all kings of Judah. **2 Kings 20:21** tells us that Manasseh was the son of Hezekiah and succeeded him as king. So, we already know that Isaiah's prophecies ended when Manasseh came into power after Hezekiah. Logically, we can ask ourselves whether it is likely that a man who proclaimed the word of the Lord for the reigns of four straight kings would have suddenly just decided to stop for any reason other than his own death. Prophets of the Lord didn't plan for retirement! Plus, **Isaiah 6:11-13** tells us that God sent Isaiah to prophesy until Judah is forsaken and ruined and the Lord has sent everyone far away. As we look further into the story, that piece of information becomes important.

The reign of Hezekiah lasts from **2 Kings 18-20**, and during this time, Hezekiah seems to accept the prophecies of Isaiah. Hezekiah trusts, follows, and seeks the word of the Lord. In **2 Kings 20**, he becomes very ill and Isaiah tells him that God says he is going to die (**v. 1**). Hezekiah pleads with God to remember his faithfulness and heal him, and God tells Isaiah to go back and tell him that God has heard his prayer and will add fifteen more years to his life (**vv. 2-6**). Isaiah speaks everything God commands and then even tells

Hezekiah how to treat his condition and also reveals the sign that God has given to show him he will be healed (**vv. 7-11**).

After this, Hezekiah accepts envoys sent from the king of Babylon and essentially shows off everything in his kingdom. He doesn't realize how foolish of a move this is until Isaiah declares that God has spoken and that one day, everything Hezekiah has shown off to the envoys will be carried off to Babylon and some of his own biological descendants will be taken as captives and made eunuchs there (**vv. 12-18**). Certainly, this is common sense. If you boast about your wealth to a pagan country who has the means and the ruthlessness to attack you and take it for themselves, you can expect that they'll come for it at some point. Hezekiah doesn't seem to be too alarmed by this because he figures it will happen after he is long gone.

After Hezekiah died, Manasseh took over and "did evil in the eyes of the Lord" (**2 Kings 21:2**). The rest of **2 Kings 21** goes on to tell us the evils that Manasseh committed, but **verse 16** is where we specifically see that he "shed so much innocent blood that he filled Jerusalem from end to end." It's not difficult to surmise that Isaiah was likely one of those innocents who was killed, especially since he was so prominent during Hezekiah's reign and we never hear from him again chronologically after this.

You might be wondering what Isaiah's faithfulness and willingness to speak the word of the Lord truly accomplished. Well, **2 Chronicles 33:1-20** gives us another view of Manasseh's reign. **Verses 11-13** show us that what Isaiah had prophesied to Hezekiah in the last known prophecy of his that we have outside of the book that bears his name came true! Manasseh, obviously a biological descendant of Hezekiah, is taken captive to Babylon after his kingdom is attacked. He likely knew of Isaiah's words about this and may have murdered him over that specific prophecy, yet now he realized that it came true. Manasseh humbled himself before the Lord and the Lord rescued him and brought him back to his home and kingdom. "Then Manasseh knew that the Lord is God" (**v. 13**). This changed everything for Manasseh and he spent the rest of his reign and life worshipping and following God, even while his people continued to sin.

Like William Wallace, Isaiah stayed loyal to his cause even to his death. Neither of them wanted to die and each of them tried to avoid it with all they could. Wallace had a wife who had been murdered and spoke of a desire to have a home and children and peace. **Isaiah 8:1-4** tells us that the prophet had a wife and at least one child. I'm sure he dreamed of living happily ever after with them, but God commanded him to speak truth and he never abandoned it, even though he knew it could cost him his life. In the end, his willingness to proclaim God's word planted a seed in Manasseh that caused him to turn back to the Lord when it came true. Isaiah may have met an awful end to this life, but he is surely counted among the faithful heroes who chose to die being right with God rather than live in opposition to Him. May we boldly follow his example if it ever comes to it in our lives.

CHAPTER 40
THE FAITH OF AHIMELEK

There is an old legal saying with an unknown original source that goes like this: "If you have the facts on your side, pound the facts. If you have the law on your side, pound the law. If you have neither on your side, pound the table." Clearly, this would lead to a lot of anger and pounding regardless of the actual truth. I remember my first day in class when I started college in the criminal justice program and one of the professors said, "The criminal justice system is a game, and the goal of the game is to win." In other words, he and many other professors wanted us to know up front that it's not really about the truth, but how you can best navigate the system to achieve your desired result.

Despite this way of the world, the Christian faith tells us no pounding is needed. Jesus himself said, "So if the Son sets you free, you will be free indeed" (**John 8:36**). If you are on the side of the truth and have been set free by the Lord, then literally nothing else can take you captive. There is a little-known man in the Bible who showed his faith by doing what he knew the Lord would want him to do, and when it was clear that it would ultimately cost him his life, he simply stood by the truth.

In **Hebrews 11:37**, we see that some of the faithful heroes of the past "were killed by the sword." God's people went through several dark periods in their history when His servants were intensely persecuted. One of those periods was when King Ahab and his wife Jezebel were slaughtering the Lord's prophets and Elijah spent much of his time on the run but still boldly spoke God's word. Another time was when eighty-five priests, along with their families and livestock, were killed with the sword by Doeg the Edomite at the command of King Saul in the town of Nob (**1 Samuel 22**). One of those priests was Ahimelek and he is our next hero of the faith.

Ahimelek became part of God's story when David, who had been anointed as the next king of Israel, had to flee because the reigning king, Saul, had become hell-bent on killing him. Since the Bible is in part a history book, it helps to know the context of what happened to Ahimelek and the other priests. Saul was the first king of Israel when the people demanded a king to lead them so that they could be like the other nations (**1 Samuel 8**). Initially, Saul had the Spirit of the Lord on his side and gave credit to the Lord when a battle was won. As time went on, however, he walked away from the Lord and became obsessed with self-preservation. He was afraid to take on Goliath in **1 Samuel 17** despite the fact that he was bigger and badder than anyone else in all of Israel. God anointed David as Saul's eventual successor and David proved himself to the people by killing Goliath.

After David's victory and sudden rise to fame, Saul became increasingly jealous of him and tried to protect his throne at all costs, even if it meant killing David who he knew was innocent. He tried to kill him several times, but the Lord kept David safe and he was able to escape. David then had to flee for his life and ended up going several different places, one of which was Nob (**1 Samuel 21**). There, David went to the right place when he sensed that he was in trouble - the house of the Lord. That's when he met Ahimelek, the priest at Nob. The story can be found in **1 Samuel 21:2-9**. David lied to Ahimelek, pretending that Saul had sent him and other men on a secret mission when in reality he was completely alone and running from the king himself. David desperately needed food so he asked Ahimelek to give him whatever he has to eat.

This is our first look at the heart of Ahimelek. As a priest, he had certain customs to follow regarding the "consecrated bread" that was kept at the house of the Lord for the priests. But here, there was a human need right in front of him. In giving David the bread, Ahimelek went against the priestly customs but did not go against God's word. God never said that ONLY priests should eat the consecrated bread; that part, while logical, was an addition to God's word.

We must never put our interpretations or applications of what God said on par with what He ACTUALLY said. Jesus spoke of Ahimelek's example as the Pharisees questioned his disciples for picking heads of grain on the Sabbath when they were hungry in

Matthew 12:1-8. He used it to make the point that human need is more important than religious tradition. Jesus' words show us that Ahimelek was to be commended for putting his faith in the Lord over traditions and customs.

In addition to the bread, Ahimelek also gave David the very sword that he had previously used to kill Goliath. Unfortunately for Ahimelek, Doeg the Edomite witnessed all of the help that Ahimelek gave to David under the impression that David was on a mission from the king. Later, in **1 Samuel 22:9-10**, this eyewitness evidence sealed the fate of Ahimelek. Doeg reported to Saul, who was already off his rocker, that he saw Ahimelek helping David, whom Saul continued to intentionally refer to as "the son of Jesse" just to remind everyone that David was just a little man from a poor family. Saul then asked Ahimelek and many other priests why they would conspire against him. Ahimelek's response is listed in **1 Samuel 22:14-15**, where he simply stood by the truth, which was that he clearly knew nothing of the conspiracy. He praised David to Saul, showing that he truly did not know Saul wanted to kill him, and also admitted to helping and praying for David other times, which revealed that he believed David's lie that Saul had sent him on a mission.

Ahimelek's defense was the honest truth. Once he had spoken it, he simply asked the king to not falsely accuse him or his family. We don't hear of another word from Ahimelek as Saul had already made up his mind to have him killed. **Verses 16-19** that follow tell us that he, his family, and most of his town were put to death by Doeg. Ahimelek did what was right in the eyes of the Lord and his death could be blamed on David's lies as much as Saul's anger. But in the end, Ahimelek valued love for a human in need over religious tradition and valued standing firm in the truth over his own life.

While he is not mentioned by name in **Hebrews 11**, the faith of he and the other priests at Nob was known to Jesus and the believers that came after him. Ahimelek's life ended when he was killed by the sword, but even today his example urges us to put the needs of others above our traditions and to let the truth stand on its own when we are falsely accused. If you are facing either of those dilemmas in your life today, learn from this man of faith.

CHAPTER 41
THE FAITH OF JOHN THE BAPTIST

"Imagine how much more we could get done in the church if no one cared who got the credit." (author unknown)

The above quote was brought back to my attention when I received life ordination as a minister in the Churches of God, General Conference denomination. A wonderful woman from my church surprised me by knitting some of my favorite quotes onto a pillow as a gift to commemorate the occasion. When I saw this quote and two others, I asked what in the world would have made her think those were specifically my favorites. Little did I know that once you put something on your Facebook profile and don't ever look at it again, others might still find it!

I signed up for Facebook in 2009 and immediately picked quotes as my "favorites" that were important to me at that time. Nine years later, I didn't remember the above quote or its source, which was likely a random seminary book I had to read. Nevertheless, reflecting on the quote makes me think of so many of the heroes of the faith we've been studying who sought the rewards of eternal life rather than temporary fame and fortune.

For the second time in this book, I'm going to veer away from those that the writer of Hebrews was likely talking about and discuss someone of whom the New Testament believers would have been aware even if they didn't have the writings that we now have. In **Hebrews 11:37**, the writer tells us some of the faithful "went about in sheepskins and goatskins, destitute, persecuted and mistreated." This description could probably best be applied to Elijah from the Old Testament, but we already discussed his faith in regards to escaping the edge of the sword. The question would then be whether there is someone else who fits this description. It just so happens that a man who entered the scene in the New Testament was just like Elijah, so much so that Jesus himself referred to this man, John the Baptist, as "the Elijah who was to come" (**Matthew 11:14**).

John the Baptist, who was related to Jesus through their mothers (**Luke 1:36**), served as a forerunner whose mission it was to prepare the way for the Lord. This means he went around preaching and proclaiming that the kingdom of heaven was near and it was time for people to "repent" (**Matthew 3:2**). Matthew tells us in **3:3** that John the Baptist fulfilled a prophecy from **Isaiah 40:3** that said there would be one in the wilderness who would call for people to get prepared for the Lord and "make straight paths for him." That isn't the only prophecy John fulfilled. **Malachi 3:1** tells us that God will send a "messenger" ahead of the Lord and **Malachi 4:5** specifically says that God will send "the prophet Elijah" before the day of the Lord. Elijah the Tishbite, the man who confronted Ahab and Jezebel, was long gone at this point, so the prophecies had to be talking about someone else, and Jesus confirmed that John the Baptist was he.

Now, what kind of living circumstances do you think a man who spent his time in the wilderness would have to endure? While he wasn't specifically forced to wear "sheepskins and goatskins," he did wear "clothes made of camel's hair" and "his food was locusts and wild honey" (**Matthew 3:4**). The big question is, "Why?" Well, Luke's gospel account tells us that the wilderness is where the word of the Lord came to John (**Luke 3:2**). How many of us receive the word of the Lord and then try to arrange our circumstances to our liking so that we can "comfortably" do what God has asked of us? That's certainly not what John the Baptist did. The word came to him in the wilderness, so he began to preach IN THE WILDERNESS. **Luke 3:3** says that "he went into all the country around the Jordan, preaching a baptism of repentance for the forgiveness of sins."

John knew what God had called him to do and preached around the Jordan River because that's where he baptized those who came. There wasn't time to waste. The kingdom was near. If he was going to preach true repentance and people were going to want to respond, the quickest and most outward way to show it was by being baptized. This was a public confession of the inward change and it happened IMMEDIATELY.

So, what exactly was he talking about when he told people to repent? I once wrote a 10-page paper on this one word in seminary and I learned that the Greek word is from the root *metanoeo*, which is a combination of *meta*, meaning "against," and *noeo*, which means "to think." This tells us that when John, and later Jesus, urged the crowds to repent, they are talking about literally changing their ways, which begins with a complete change in thinking. It could be said that repentance is literally going against one's current thought or understanding. As people encountered John the Baptist and heard about the coming of the Messiah, they were moved to completely change their thoughts and ways and do a complete 180-degree turn. John told them that the water baptism was a symbol of what was to come - the baptism of the Holy Spirit that happens only through Jesus.

John the Baptist became quite the popular figure as more and more came to him, but he remembered his mission and didn't seek anything more. Even as some thought he was the Messiah, he reminded them that he wouldn't even be worthy to carry the sandals of the true Messiah (**Matthew 3:11**). He didn't seek a building to fit a megachurch, didn't ask for a large salary with good benefits, and didn't demand respect and authority. He simply hung out in the wilderness, munching on locusts and wearing camel's hair, and preached what God gave him to preach.

When specific people like soldiers and tax collectors asked what repentance would look like for them, John was direct in telling them how to live rightly (**Luke 3:12-14**). He urged people to not just feel sorry for their sins, but to confess them and to bear fruit that shows the change that came from repentance (**Luke 3:8**). His message was well-received by most, but not all. Because he was so focused on speaking truth and not what was in it for him, he boldly rebuked King Herod for marrying his brother's wife among other wicked acts, which unfortunately landed John in prison for the rest of his life until Herod had him killed (**Luke 3:19-20**).

John the Baptist was certainly a copycat of Elijah in many ways. He lived in humble circumstances, boldly called out the wickedness of a pagan ruler, and urged repentance from God's people. But John the Baptist said something that, to our knowledge, no one else did. Despite his boldness in challenging wicked authority, his response to Jesus was marked by humility like no one else had seen. When some of his disciples complained that people were going to Jesus rather than him, he simply reminded them that he was not the Messiah and was given only the joy of preparing the way for Him (**John 3:26-29**). Then, he spoke the words by which we should remember and emulate him. Speaking of Jesus, he said, "He must become greater; I must become less" (**John 3:30**).

Are you willing to become "less" so that you can make Jesus "greater" in the eyes of the world? One thing's for sure: you wouldn't be able to care who gets the credit. Let John's faith and his willingness to accept his role in God's story of redemption speak to you today. Use his example as a catalyst for repentance and humility in your own life.

CHAPTER 42
THE FAITH OF OBADIAH

Irena Sendler was a woman who risked everything to save the innocent and oppressed. She valued God's standard of justice, mercy, and humility (**Micah 6:8**) over the current laws of the land. Her "land" happened to be Nazi-occupied Warsaw, Poland during the time of the Holocaust. Irena actually did what many of us would like to think we'd do if we were in her situation. She used her position as a social worker to rescue some 2,500 Jewish children by smuggling them out of the Warsaw ghetto, giving them fake identities, and arranging for them to receive the care and shelter they needed in safe places. She had an understanding, just like Queen Esther in the Bible, that God had probably given her the position she had for such a time as the one she faced.

Irena is quoted by Wikipedia as saying, "Every child saved with my help is the justification of my existence on this Earth, and not a title to glory." She did not see it as something for which she could boast, but as the ONLY reasonable choice for a true follower of God to make in that situation. She risked everything to save those children and endured severe torture and imprisonment, but never gave up the names or locations of the children she rescued. Irena Sendler is a true, contemporary hero of the faith.

Her story reminds me of a man from the Old Testament, who is the final specific hero of the faith I will address in this book. As we come toward the end of **Hebrews 11**, the writer tells us that "the world was not worthy" of the faithful heroes about whom he's been writing (**v. 38**). In other words, the collective group of the despised, mistreated, and martyred servants of God were of greater worth than all the rest of humanity combined. The world did not see them as valuable and likely forgot about them after they were gone, but the writer reminds us that God will not forget about them and neither should we if we want to know what it's like to live out our faith in the midst of the trials we face today. But then, after making what appears to be a concluding statement about the heroes of the faith, the writer surprisingly adds one more description of them: "They wandered in deserts and mountains, living in caves and in holes in the ground" (v. 38).

We can't be sure why the writer came back to this, but it's worth noting that two of the most well-known heroes from the Old Testament, David and Elijah, would BOTH fit this statement. Both men followed the Lord and were forced to live as fugitives as the evil kings leading God's people sought to kill them. Since we've already discussed those men in this book, I want to turn your attention to a lesser known faithful hero, but one who still played a major role in the history of faith and specifically in the story of Elijah.

The man's name is Obadiah. Now, we know that someone named Obadiah wrote a book of prophecy in the Old Testament, but we can't be sure which one it was because there are numerous "Obadiahs" mentioned other places in the Old Testament. The name means "servant of Yahweh" and that's no surprise because the Obadiah of Elijah's day certainly fits that moniker. You can find his role in the story in **1 Kings 18:2-16**, which are the verses directly preceding Elijah's confrontation with the prophets of Baal.

This is where I can begin to draw similarities between Obadiah and Irena Sendler. Obadiah was the palace administrator under the evil King Ahab. This means he was in a unique position to work for justice even as the maniacal king and his crazy wife Jezebel were slaughtering many of the Lord's prophets. We might think that he should have stood up to them, but remember that even Jesus told His followers to be "as shrewd as snakes and as innocent as doves" (**Matthew 10:16**).

Sometimes, we're too quick to leave bad situations. We see discomfort for ourselves or evil all around us and we conclude that God must want us to leave. But maybe God wants us to be the change agent, or maybe he just wants us to use the platform he has given us to do his work in some way. This is a perfect example of understanding what it means to be in the world but not of the world (**John 17:15-16**).

Obadiah was put in a position, within an administration where he clearly didn't agree with the rulers, to do God's work even at great personal risk. **1 Kings 18:3-4** tells us that he was a "devout believer in the Lord" who "had taken a hundred prophets and hidden them in two caves, fifty in each, and had supplied them with food and water." I understand that all indications are that Obadiah himself did not have to go live in a cave, so the writer of Hebrews was likely talking about the great faith of the prophets who trusted him. There's no doubt that they also are to be commended. But they faced a certain death had it not been for Obadiah risking his life for them.

Obadiah's faith didn't end there. As the story continues, he is commanded by Ahab to go look for grass to feed their mules and horses because they are nearing starvation during the major famine across the land. As he follows the command of his superior, he is out walking and stumbles across Elijah (**v. 7**). Elijah tells him to go and tell Ahab that he has found Elijah. Obadiah, knowing that Ahab has been searching all over God's green earth looking for Elijah to kill him, understandably has a brief moment of trepidation. He is certain that the Spirit of God is leading Elijah and worries that if he goes and tells Ahab that Elijah is there and then Ahab cannot find him, he'll be called to account with his life (**vv. 9-14**). Elijah simply gives him the assurance that he would present himself to Ahab later that day, because we all know that if you're following the Lord wholeheartedly there really is nothing and no one to fear.

After that, we see that Obadiah puts his faith in God and in the promise from Elijah and spills the beans to Ahab. He had already been willing to die if he got caught hiding the 100 prophets, so why not keep leaving his life up to God anyway? Obadiah's part of the story ends there. We know what took place between Elijah and Ahab after that, but we don't know what part, if any, Obadiah continued to have. We don't know how much longer he served Ahab, or whether he was alive or dead when Ahab finally got what was coming to him. What we do know about Obadiah is that he was faithful. God doesn't call us to worry about the results. We can trust those to Him. He just calls us to be faithful.

Obadiah was faithful in smuggling prophets into caves just like Irena Sendler was faithful in smuggling children into homes. Both individuals didn't stop there but continued to supply those they had rescued with their daily needs. Both of them put doing what was right in God's eyes ahead of loyalty to an evil and wicked man.

Are you willing to live like these individuals, or do you constantly seek whatever is most comfortable and then try to tell yourself and others that it's what God wants? What He truly wants is obedience and faithfulness regardless of the comfort level. He has put you on this earth for a reason. You do not exist unto yourself alone, but you have a purpose and a responsibility to use whatever platform or position He has given you to bless, love, and serve others. What's stopping you and why? Surrender it to the Lord this very day!

CHAPTER 43
THE FAITH OF LOGAN, CLARA, AND EVANGELINE

I bet that sounds pretty arrogant, doesn't it? I mean, who in the world would write a chapter about their own faith in a series about the heroes of the faith? Well, it was suggested to me by another writer based on what has taken place in my life and I feel it's appropriate for several reasons. First, I don't think that any of the "heroes" of the faith would have considered themselves as such. They did and experienced great things by faith not in their own abilities or merit, but through a righteous, just, and loving God. In their own eyes, they weren't even almost heroes, but were simply doing what they knew was right in God's eyes even when it was difficult. Secondly, God honored their faith even though they were ordinary human beings who struggled with sins just like we do. Third, those individuals who were faithful had no special power to see the future. When they chose to be faithful, they had no idea how God would use their circumstances to reveal himself to others.

Each of these things ought to be true about our lives as well. I want to conclude this book by sharing a little bit about how God has been faithful in my own life, and then turn the page toward the challenge that lies before all Christians to stand firm in the faith He has given us.

My wife Clara and I welcomed our first child into this world on June 19, 2018. We chose not to find out the gender of our child ahead of time, but we are now blessed to be the parents of our precious daughter, Evangeline Myra Ames. As I think back on the faith of my wife and I over the course of our relationship, there have been so many times that we struggled, sinned, or frankly didn't even stop and consider what God would have us do. But God, who is always faithful (**1 Thessalonians 5:24**), has continued to do his work even when we weren't concerned with Him.

Clara and I did not always honor God in our relationship with the way we viewed and treated one another. However, we made the decision of commitment in 2015 and were married on July 2, 2016. If you've followed my writings on the Worldview Warriors blog over the years, you may remember that I took a season away from Worldview Warriors during that time.

Even after we said our vows, we learned that marriage is a blessing but not always easy. We both struggled with where God had us in our jobs in Ohio and wrestled with any changes he would want us to make. God turned our discontentment into an opportunity to trust Him when we began to consider moving to York, Pennsylvania, which was only 40 minutes from where I grew up and about two hours from where she did. I was offered a lead pastor position at a local church in PA and we decided to take it. I can certainly say that we prayed about it, but I'm not sure how much we listened. Like many of you, I presume, we do a lot of talking in our prayers but find it hard to sit and silently listen. Yet, God was faithful anyway.

We made the trip back to PA on June 19, 2017. If you're keeping track, that's exactly one year before our little angel arrived in this world. We grieved having to leave what was comfortable in Ohio and bid farewell to the many friends we had made during our time there, but we saw many ways that God was with us during the process. From the many people who helped us with the move on both ends to the fact that God provided a job in PA for my wife where she got to help people who struggle with mental illness from a faith-based perspective, we've experienced God's goodness all the way.

Then came the biggest blessing of all. We decided that while we were open to having children if it be God's will for us, we would do very little to "plan" it. It would be totally up to God if and when it happens. We found out in October that Clara was expecting and, to say the least, she had a blessed pregnancy with very little sickness and no complications.

Evangeline graced us with her presence exactly a year after we made our giant step of faith. She is the best gift of all. We chose the name Evangeline for two reasons. The first is that it is part of Clara's family history, but the second is that her name comes from the Greek εὐαγγέλιον or *euangélion*, which simply means "the good news." We know that she is a blessing from above and that she represents the good news of Jesus in our lives. We don't deserve her and we don't always know what she needs or how to best care for her, but she puts her faith in us daily just as we put our faith in God daily.

One of the most important aspects of faith for any Christian is knowing that you need more of it. Read the story of the man whose son was demon-possessed until Jesus healed him in **Mark 9:14-29**. The man declared that he believed, yet still asked Jesus to help him overcome his unbelief. That's where we all should often find ourselves, admitting that we need Jesus' help to fully trust Him. A person who has NO faith cannot utter these words, for it is only by faith that one can realize that they need more of it.

We'll never consider ourselves heroes of faith, and most days we just hope to make more right choices than wrongs ones in God's eyes. But the more we trust in Him, the more His providence is obvious in our lives. We pray that Evangeline will not only strengthen our faith and dependence on God but also be an example to the world around her.

What steps is God asking you to take that make you afraid today? Think about the endless possibilities of how He might just be waiting to bless your socks off until you trust Him a little bit. Once you've practiced trusting Him a little bit, then move on to trusting Him more and more. Not everything will be easy, but God is faithful even when we are not and you will never regret depending on Him.

CHAPTER 44
THE FAITH OF THE CHURCH

As our nation celebrated our 242nd year of independence in 2018, I found myself thinking about how many people must have dreamt about it and pursued it only to never fully experience it. We in America certainly take it for granted because we've all been born into freedom and have never known what it's like to be oppressed by a nation or a government. But that's not how it was for the original patriots who risked and in many cases gave their lives for this cause. That being said, we still have a role and a responsibility today to continue that cause for two reasons: 1) so that those who come after us will continue to enjoy the freedoms we have enjoyed, and 2) so that the sacrifices and efforts of those who went before us would not be wasted. In other words, it's up to US to carry the torch of freedom and keep it burning.

When you think about it, this has been true about any noble cause that has ever existed. Other than Jesus dying for the sins of the whole world on the cross, God never intended for one person to do it all. Martin Luther King, Jr. didn't begin the Civil Rights Movement (Rosa Parks and others came before him) and he certainly was assassinated before he got to experience the fullness of the freedom and desegregation that he dreamt of. Others had to keep the torch burning. Robert Gould Shaw (portrayed by Matthew Broderick in the movie *Glory*) was a white man who fought and died in the Civil War for the cause of freedom for slaves. His torch would have burned out if others didn't keep it going.

It's true about ministry as well. I have a friend who is a missionary in Ecuador working to help develop pastors and churches there who are ministering to the natives. The organization he works for put out a publication that states the work of evangelism in Ecuador began with Jim Elliot and the men who were with him in 1956. They were all martyred, but the seeds they planted were watered by others and now missionaries and native Christians are beginning to reap the harvest there.

It reminds me of the words of the writer at the end of **Hebrews 11**. As I have taken you through faithful hero by faithful hero in the entirety of this book, I pray that these examples of faith have ignited a fire within you to carry on their torch. That's what the writer of Hebrews also desired.

In **Hebrews 11:39-40**, he reminds us, "These were all commended for their faith, yet none of them received what had been promised, since God had planned something better for us so that only together with us would they be made perfect." The idea of being made perfect is actually that they are made "complete." In other words, all these heroes of the faith that we've talked about in this book had a faith that was not yet made complete. Now, that's not to say THEIR faith was incomplete. They followed God with boldness and total dependence on Him. But the faith to which they devoted themselves was based on something God had promised but had not yet come to fruition. In that sense, the universal, Christian faith was not made complete until Jesus came, lived, died on the cross, and was raised to life again.

What does this mean for you, me, and all believers and followers of Jesus? The writer tells us as the next chapter begins. In **Hebrews 12:1**, we see the word "therefore," which directly refers back to every single mention of a hero of the faith, as well as the very last words from **chapter 11**. The writer tells us that we have some advantages that these faithful heroes didn't have. The Church (capitalized to signify all Christians past, present, and future) ought to consider what each and every one of these faithful heroes did and how they stood firm in the incomplete faith that had not yet seen the arrival of the Messiah.

Hebrews 12:1 calls these heroes "witnesses," which is actually from the Greek *marturos* and is where we get the English term "martyr." You see, a martyr isn't just someone who loses their life; it's what all Christians are called to be to the extent that God asks of us. I might have to give up my life or I might only be asked to give up my desire for popularity and approval of those who would have me compromise the truth to obtain those things. Either way, every follower of Jesus must decide whether they will stand firm in their faith or be on shaky ground in something else.

The writer of Hebrews then tells the Church that, since we are surrounded by these witnesses and their stories - an advantage many of the faithful didn't have as they stood out among the unfaithful - we have reason to get rid of the things in our lives that hinder us from faith and avoid the sins that ensnare us (**v. 1**). He says we ought to persevere in the "race marked out for us" even when it's difficult. The way to do that is what the writer explains is another advantage that we have - we can "fix our eyes on Jesus, the pioneer and perfecter of our faith" (**Hebrews 12:2**).

None of the ancient heroes of our faith described in **Hebrews 11** could fix their eyes on Jesus because He had not yet come! They knew of Him only in the sense that they believed in the promise, but it was still something they could only imagine. To our knowledge, the name "Jesus" was not revealed to any of them. So, when the writer mentions our Savior by His human name, only those who have come after Him can find strength from His endurance.

We are reminded in **Hebrews 12:2-3** of what exactly our Savior endured. The cross was not just physically painful but also publicly shaming. Yet, Jesus "scorned its shame and sat down at the right hand of the throne of God." The author of Hebrews tells us that when we are struggling, we should consider not only all of those other faithful heroes, but the most faithful of them all - Jesus of Nazareth. If we consider all that He went through and endured, as well as His great reward of sitting at the right hand of God (the highest position of honor there is), we "will not grow weary and lose heart" (**v. 3**).

The heroes of the faith in the past chose to stand firm even though they had yet to see what was promised. If they could endure so much without seeing the promise come true, how much more reason do we have to continue to keep the torch of faith burning, knowing that God has been faithful in keeping His promises? If you are part of the Church, you have this responsibility for the next generation.

I don't know what God will ask you to endure, but I know that you have examples right in front of your eyes of those who have endured and have overcome even more. By the same faith that was central to the lives of so many before you, you can reason that God is bigger than your problems, that He has a plan, and that following Him even when circumstances seem to be against you is more logical than rejecting Him and His commands.

As I said at the beginning of this book, faith in God is not blind. Follow the evidence, which includes all these faithful stories before you, and make your choice to stand firm in that faith. May God bless and reward you as you do!

Equipping Students to Impact This Generation
For Jesus Christ

www.WorldviewWarriors.org

Worldview Warriors
P.O. Box 681
Findlay, OH 45839

info@worldviewwarriors.org
(419) 835-2777

We provide free weekly resources available to use in
personal study, small groups, Sunday school classes, sermons, etc.

Contact us to book Logan Ames or one of our other speakers
for interviews or your next event!

Find us on Facebook
www.Facebook.com/WorldviewWarriors

DONOTKEEPSILENT

Speaking out the name of Jesus Christ in action and in word

DO NOT KEEP SILENT

We are a talk radio show that plays great music as well for those
wanting to grow in their relationship with Christ

**90.1 FM - WXML in Upper Sandusky, OH area
Sunday evenings from 7pm - 9pm**

**Radio4Him online
Wednesday evenings from 7pm - 9pm**

We have a 2-hour program and a 30-minute program available

DoNotKeepSilent.com

Facebook.com/DoNotKeepSilent

Made in the USA
Middletown, DE
12 March 2019